BUILD4SKILLS

INTEGRATING TRAINEESHIPS INTO ADB-SUPPORTED INFRASTRUCTURE PROJECTS

A HANDBOOK FOR PROJECT PROCESSING TEAMS AND PROJECT IMPLEMENTATION UNITS

SECOND EDITION

ASIAN DEVELOPMENT BANK

CONTENTS

TABLES, FIGURES, AND BOXES

BOXES

PREFACE

Build4Skills began with a simple idea: Why not use construction sites supported by the Asian Development Bank (ADB) to provide work-based training to local youth? Given the proven effectiveness of work-based training in getting young people into labor markets and the large infrastructure portfolio of ADB that could be leveraged, the Build4Skills idea appeared as a potential waiting to be explored.

Consequently, ADB entered into a partnership with the German Federal Ministry for Economic Cooperation and Development (BMZ) and its implementing agency, the German Agency for International Cooperation (GIZ), bringing together leading development organizations in the fields of infrastructure development and vocational education. The aim of the cooperation was to develop a scalable approach for integrating traineeships into infrastructure projects.

Build4Skills traineeships were introduced in ADB-supported urban and social infrastructure projects in Mongolia and Pakistan, jointly coordinated by staff from ADB and GIZ, one of whom was seconded to ADB headquarters. The activities proved that clients have a demand for the approach and can be feasibly integrated on ADB-supported construction sites.

As a second step, lessons learned from the activities were translated into an operational model that can be replicated in any future ADB-supported infrastructure projects. During the development of the operational model, discussions revolved around (i) how projects can cost-efficiently process traineeships, (ii) how traineeships can become a procurement requirement, (iii) how these can be sustainably funded, and (iv) what safeguards should be considered. These questions were explored in a cross-departmental dialogue. The final product, the *Build4Skills Handbook,* is a ready-to-use solution for ADB clients and project teams to cost-efficiently integrate traineeships into infrastructure projects and scale up across the ADB portfolio.

This is the second edition of the handbook incorporating new lessons learned. The pilots have shown that in-depth technical guidance for procurement practitioners on integrating traineeship requirements into civil work contracts is a critical success factor. Therefore, a new practice guide specifically aimed at procurement practitioners was developed and will be published alongside this second edition. The practice guide zooms into the procurement-related steps of the Build4Skills approach outlining in technical detail how to incorporate traineeship requirements into bidding documents and the bill of quantities, as well as manage disbursements. This second edition of the handbook was aligned with the practice guide. It still captures the

Build4Skills operational model in its entirety, outlining all steps from project preparation to implementation. New to the second edition are cross-references to the new practice guide, a greater emphasis on the responsibility of contractors in implementation, and detailed instructions on procurement were moved to the practice guide, including the template traineeship contract requirements.

The Build4Skills approach demonstrates how interagency cooperation can create new and innovative solutions to global challenges, and this handbook is a testimony to the advantages of strategic cooperation between development partners.

ACKNOWLEDGMENTS

The publication was prepared by Alexander Tsironis, education specialist at the Human and Social Development Sector Office of the Asian Development Bank (ADB).

Special thanks are extended to ADB colleagues Celita Janyna Rhor, principal procurement specialist; Jenny Yan Yee Chu, procurement specialist; Kevin Moore, principal procurement specialist; Prasath Sanjeewa, procurement specialist; Philipp Kalpaxis, senior procurement specialist; Eisuke Tajima, principal education specialist; and Arnaud Heckmann, principal portfolio management specialist; and Anna Kontny, education specialist at the German Agency for International Cooperation (GIZ), for providing constructive feedback and suggestions as peer reviewers. Critical insights on safeguards were provided by Felix Nii Tettey Oku, senior social development specialist (safeguards), and Aida Khalil Gomez, principal safeguard specialist, while input on results management was given by Mirza Nadia Bashnin, senior results management specialist, and Vivian Santos Francisco, senior results management officer, all with ADB.

The handbook is based on pilot experiences in Mongolia and Pakistan, where colleagues, partners, and project offices have supported the implementation of activities and participated in dialogues about the experiences reflected in the handbook. Appreciation goes to ADB's Bisma Husen, Rubina Shaheen, Davaasuren Terbish, Avirmed Dangaa, and Per Borjegren, as well as to GIZ's Odbayar Dashzeveg, Gurtsog Budkhand, Sharjeel Farooq, Waqas Waheed, and Safdar Ali Khan.

Support in the finalization of this publication was provided by ADB colleagues Dorothy Geronimo, senior education officer, SG-HSD; and Maria Theresa Mercado, editor (consultant).

This publication would not have been produced without the encouragement and overall guidance of Shanti Jagannathan, director of the education practice team of the SG-HSD; Ayako Inagaki, senior director of the SG-HSD; Heike Kuhn, head of education division at the German Federal Ministry for Economic Cooperation and Development (BMZ); Birte Ifang, senior policy officer at BMZ; and Imke Kottmann, head of project at GIZ.

ABBREVIATIONS

ADB	–	Asian Development Bank
BMZ	–	Bundesministerium für wirtschaftliche Zusammenarbeit und Entwicklung (German Federal Ministry for Economic Cooperation and Development)
CWCP	–	civil works contract package
FAQs	–	frequently asked questions
GIZ	–	Deutsche Gesellschaft für Internationale Zusammenarbeit (German Agency for International Cooperation)
KPI	–	key performance indicator
PIU	–	project implementation unit
RRP	–	report and recommendation of the President
SPP	–	strategic procurement planning
TVET	–	technical and vocational education and training
WBT	–	work-based training

WHO IS THIS HANDBOOK FOR?

This step-by-step guide on integrating traineeships into Asian Development Bank (ADB)-supported infrastructure projects is for

Project team leads and team members from ADB and government, to know how to process traineeships into the project design at the project preparation stage.

Implementing agencies and project implementation units, to know how to coordinate the delivery of traineeships in cooperation with contractors during project implementation.

10 THINGS YOU SHOULD KNOW ABOUT THE BUILD4SKILLS HANDBOOK

1.	What is the Build4Skills approach	The Build4Skills approach recommends that Asian Development Bank (ADB)-supported infrastructure projects make traineeships a requirement in civil work contracts—requiring contractors to provide traineeship opportunities to local youth. The underlying idea is to create wider societal benefits through a simple change to contract requirements.
2.	Why should ADB clients consider this?	ADB clients should consider Build4Skills to (i) create additional social impact, including youth inclusion and employability, project reputation, and potentially long-term benefits to local labor markets; and (ii) align with development strategies, such as ADB Strategy 2030.[a]
3.	What is the handbook, and who is it for?	The handbook is a step-by-step guide on how to integrate traineeships into project processing (for OneADB teams) and deliver them during project implementation (for implementing agencies).
4.	Which projects can use the handbook?	Any ADB-supported infrastructure project in any sector—energy, urban, transport, water, health, and education—can use the handbook.
5.	What should ADB project teams do with the approach?	Project teams can propose to clients to integrate Build4Skills traineeships into project design. The concept is already developed for easy integration.
6.	Why deliver traineeships on construction sites?	Traineeships are proven to be effective in teaching technical skills and helping youth transition into jobs. ADB oversees a large infrastructure portfolio that can be readily leveraged for traineeship opportunities to local communities.
7.	How are traineeships integrated into projects?	The handbook suggests making traineeships a procurement requirement in selected civil works contract packages and processing them as part of regular project documents, and not as a separate technical assistance.
8.	How are traineeships funded?	The handbook suggests funding traineeships directly through the project loan by including a provisional sum, earmarked for traineeships, in the bill of quantities of civil works contract packages. This ensures easy integration, predictable costs, and sustainable funding.
9.	Why is Build4Skills a strong development practice?	Build4Skills combines important development practices including quality infrastructure, youth inclusion, social procurement, and public–private cooperation. It is also scalable, evidence-based, cross-sectoral, and cost-efficient.
10.	What is the Build4Skills Practice Guide for Procurement Practitioners?	The practice guide for procurement practitioners supplements the handbook. It describes in greater detail how traineeships are incorporated into bidding documents and disbursements managed during project implementation. It is aimed at procurement specialists, consultants, and contract managers.

[a] ADB. 2018. *Strategy 2030: Achieving a Prosperous, Inclusive, Resilient, and Sustainable Asia and the Pacific.*

1

INTRODUCTION

The Asian Development Bank (ADB) is committed to supporting its developing member countries in delivering quality and inclusive infrastructure as promoted in the ADB Strategy 2030[1] and the G20 Quality Infrastructure Investment Principles.[2] Quality infrastructure frameworks recognize that in the pursuit of the Sustainable Development Goals (SDGs), it is not sufficient to deliver just hard infrastructure—infrastructure projects must also create social impacts, such as employment, traineeships, and skills development, in the communities where they operate. Most ADB-supported infrastructure projects have the potential to provide on-the-job traineeships on their construction sites creating opportunities for youth in line with SDGs. This potential has been unexplored as there has been no structured approach on how to cost-efficiently operationalize it.

To address this gap and unlock the social impact potential of infrastructure projects for clients,[3] the ADB Human and Social Development Sector Office[4] has developed the Build4Skills approach in cooperation with the German Agency for International Cooperation (GIZ) commissioned by the German Federal Ministry for Economic Cooperation and Development (BMZ). Inspired by the German dual training system, the Build4Skills approach recommends that ADB-supported infrastructure projects make the delivery of work-based training (WBT) (Box 1) a contract requirement in civil work contracts requiring contractors to provide traineeship opportunities to local youth. The underlying opportunity is that infrastructure projects can generate wider societal benefits through a simple change to procurement requirements, resulting in significant outcomes for youth and communities.

Box 1: What Is Work-Based Training?

Work-based training refers to all forms of learning, both initial and continuous, that take place in a real-world environment. It may be referred to as traineeship, on-the-job training, apprenticeship, or internship.

Source: Author, based on Asian Development Bank. 2018. Work-Based Learning for Skills Development Explainer. *Development Asia*.

---

[1] ADB. 2018. *Strategy 2030: Achieving a Prosperous, Inclusive, Resilient, and Sustainable Asia and the Pacific.*

[2] ADB. 2021. *Supporting Quality Infrastructure in Developing Asia.* Manila; *G20 Principles for Quality Infrastructure Investment.*

[3] "Client" in the context of this handbook refers to government partners—often ministries—that ADB works with, which usually become the project executing or implementing agency in investment projects.

[4] Formerly the ADB education sector group.

The *Build4Skills Handbook* outlines how traineeships can be operationalized as part of ADB-supported infrastructure projects. It provides OneADB teams, implementing agencies, and project implementation units (PIUs) with a step-by-step guide on how to cost-effectively process and implement traineeships. OneADB teams can propose Build4Skills traineeships as an out-of-the-box project design consideration to ADB clients (Figure 1). The value added for clients is a more inclusive project design that creates tangible impact, including improved youth inclusion and employability, an improved project reputation, and potentially, local workforce productivity in the long run (Figure 1).

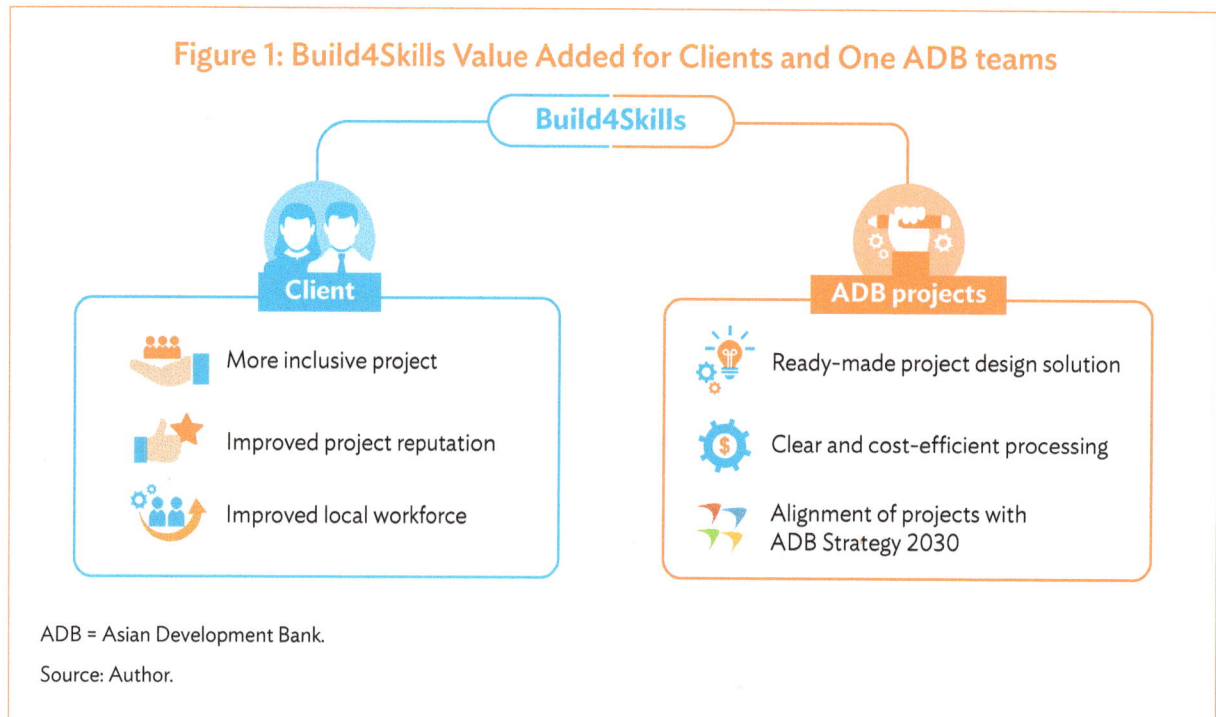

Figure 1: Build4Skills Value Added for Clients and One ADB teams

Build4Skills

Client
- More inclusive project
- Improved project reputation
- Improved local workforce

ADB projects
- Ready-made project design solution
- Clear and cost-efficient processing
- Alignment of projects with ADB Strategy 2030

ADB = Asian Development Bank.
Source: Author.

The Build4Skills approach is designed to ensure cost-efficiency and scalability. Cost-efficiency is ensured by processing Build4Skills as part of regular project processing steps, integrating it into civil work procurement, and leveraging ADB-supported construction sites as traineeships sites. The result is additional, scalable impact at minimal additional overhead. Scaling up WBT on ADB-supported construction sites across all sectors (energy, urban, transport, water, health, education) is supported by the handbook, which provides a standard operating procedure for its replication. Overall Build4Skills traineeships are an opportunity to make infrastructure project designs more inclusive (Figure 2).

The *Build4Skills Handbook* is divided into four chapters (Figure 3). Following the introduction, Chapter 2 describes the strategic relevance and impact chain of the Build4Skills approach. Chapter 3 introduces how Build4Skills traineeships seamlessly integrate into ADB project processing, procurement, and implementation. Chapter 4, the main part of the handbook, details how each step of the Build4Skills operational model can be implemented. The 5 stages and 15 implementation steps of the Build4Skills

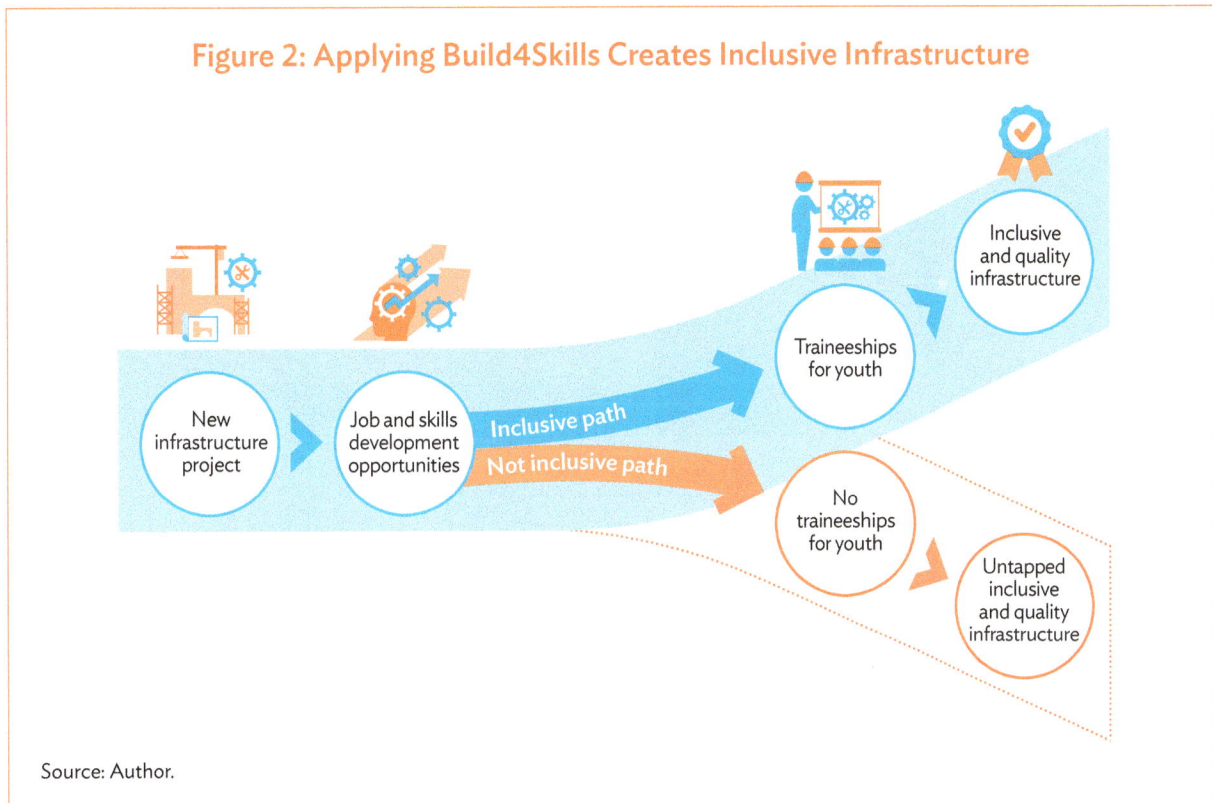

Figure 2: Applying Build4Skills Creates Inclusive Infrastructure

New infrastructure project

Job and skills development opportunities

Inclusive path

Not inclusive path

Traineeships for youth

Inclusive and quality infrastructure

No traineeships for youth

Untapped inclusive and quality infrastructure

Source: Author.

operational model are logically organized along the ADB project cycle.[5] In the Appendix, templates are provided, making the handbook an out-of-the-box solution that can be implemented directly by OneADB teams and implementing agencies.

As procurement is a critical element in the implementation of Build4Skills traineeships, the handbook is supplemented by the *Build4Skills Practice Guide for Procurement Practitioners*. Whereas the handbook outlines the entire Build4Skills approach from end-to-end, including client consultations, project processing, and implementation, the practice guide focuses exclusively on procurement-related activities of the Build4Skills approach. It provides technical details on how to procure traineeships as part of civil work contracts to guide procurement specialists and consultants when implementing steps 5 and 15 of this handbook. The practice guide is available as a linked document to the *Build4Skills Handbook* on the ADB website.[6]

---

[5] It focuses on the preparation and implementation phase of the ADB project cycle as they are most relevant for Build4Skills.
[6] ADB. 2024. *Build4Skills Practice Guide for Procurement Practitioners*.

Figure 3: Chapter Overview of Build4Skills Handbook

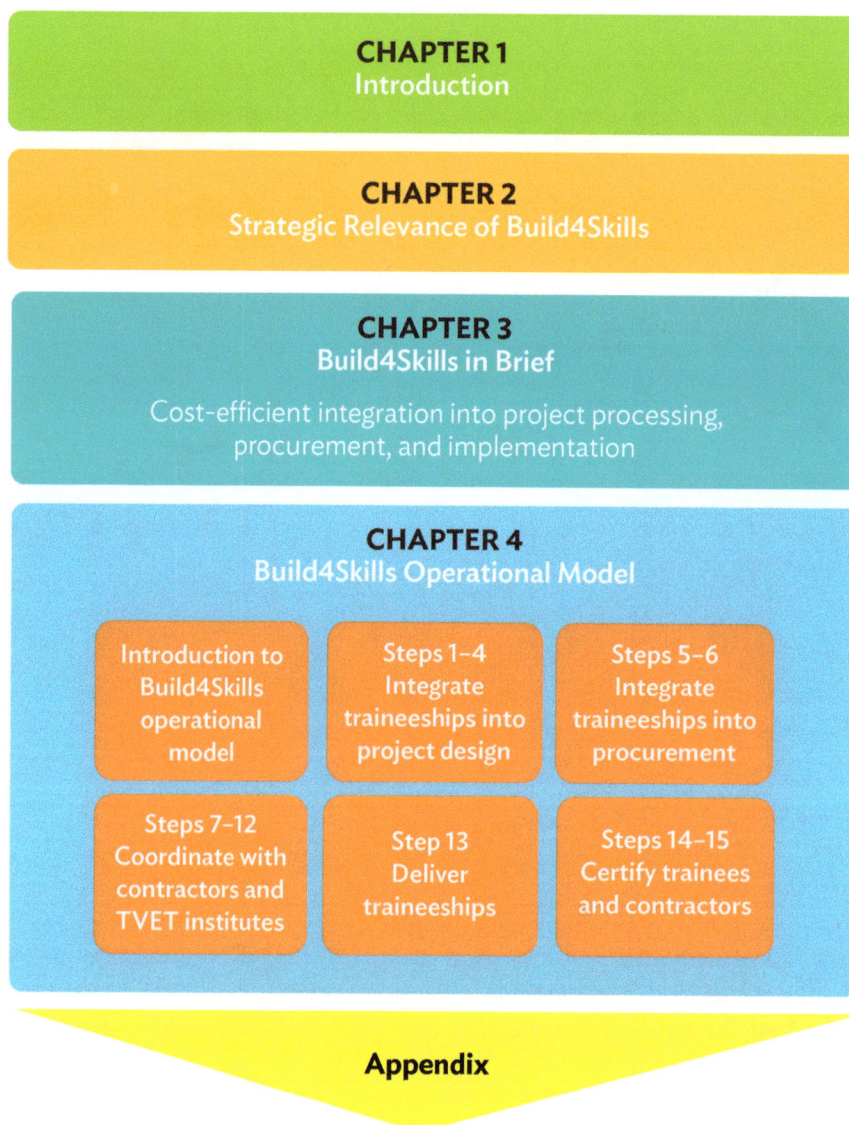

CHAPTER 1
Introduction

CHAPTER 2
Strategic Relevance of Build4Skills

CHAPTER 3
Build4Skills in Brief

Cost-efficient integration into project processing,
procurement, and implementation

CHAPTER 4
Build4Skills Operational Model

Introduction to Build4Skills operational model	Steps 1–4 Integrate traineeships into project design	Steps 5–6 Integrate traineeships into procurement
Steps 7–12 Coordinate with contractors and TVET institutes	Step 13 Deliver traineeships	Steps 14–15 Certify trainees and contractors

Appendix

TVET = technical and vocational education and training.
Source: Author.

2

STRATEGIC RELEVANCE FOR ADB AND IMPACT CHAIN OF BUILD4SKILLS

Build4Skills aligns with various ADB strategies and development agendas. Build4Skills is a response to the G20 Quality Infrastructure Investment Principles calling for more social considerations in infrastructure, which are also emphasized in ADB's *Supporting Quality Infrastructure in Developing Asia* report.[7] Moreover, creating traineeship opportunities is aligned with the operational priorities (OPs) of ADB Strategy 2030: enhanced human capital for all and quality jobs generated (OP1) and, potentially, enhanced gender equality in human development (OP2), as well as the Sustainable Development Goals (SDGs) on education (SDG 4) and decent jobs (SDG 8). By delivering traineeships through construction companies, Build4Skills follows the key recommendation of ADB's *Education Sector Directional Guide*[8] to mobilize the private sector for training delivery. Finally, the ADB *Sustainable Public Procurement: Guidance Note on Procurement*[9] highlights that public procurement can include social considerations to generate broader benefits to society. Build4Skills is one possible approach to leverage public procurement purchasing power to generate such social benefits.

Beyond strategies, the objective of Build4Skills is to create value added for clients and their beneficiaries. As depicted in the impact chain (Figure 4), Build4Skills traineeships provide benefits for different stakeholders. The youth benefit from improved employability and better chances to get into jobs with higher incomes. Clients benefit from improved project reputation and public approval. Contractors have access to formally trained and potentially more productive workers. They also have the opportunity to improve their talent management capacity in the long run. Equally, the capacity of technical and vocational education and training (TVET) institutes to cooperate with companies in WBT may also improve, which could result in more local public–private training partnerships and, eventually, in better local labor market outcomes.

---

[7] ADB. 2021. *Supporting Quality Infrastructure in Developing Asia*.

[8] ADB. 2022. *Strategy 2030 Education Sector Directional Guide*.

[9] ADB. 2021. *Sustainable Public Procurement: Guidance Note on Procurement*.

Figure 4: Impact Chain of Build4Skills Traineeships

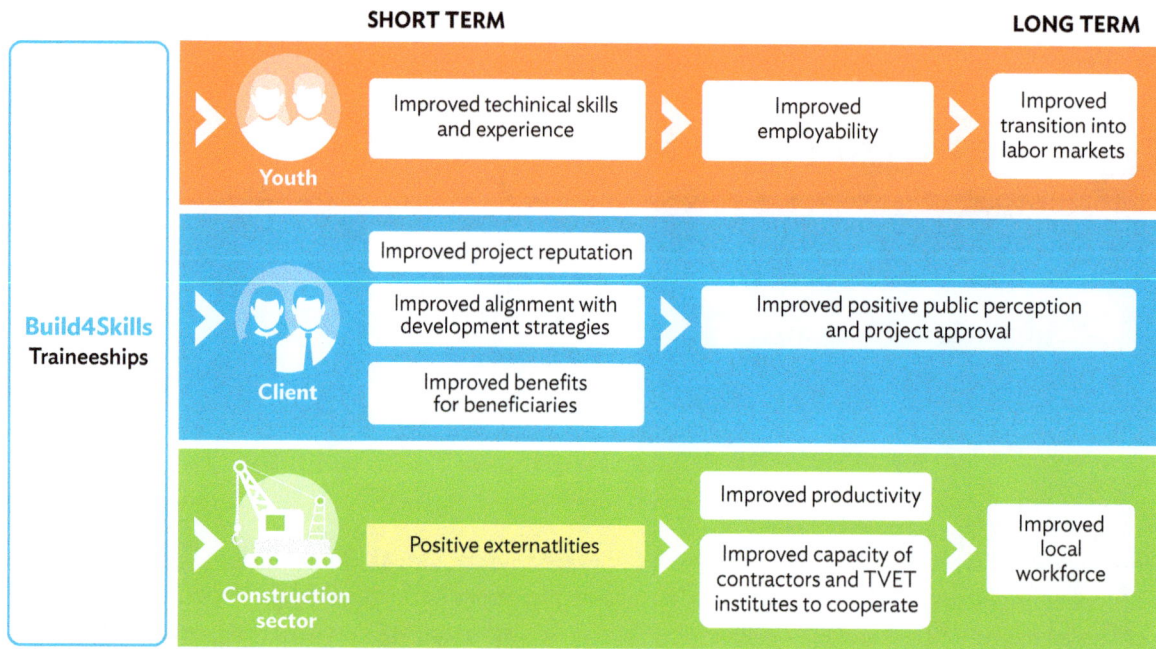

SHORT TERM   **LONG TERM**

Build4Skills Traineeships

Youth
Improved techinical skills and experience → Improved employability → Improved transition into labor markets

Client
Improved project reputation
Improved alignment with development strategies → Improved positive public perception and project approval
Improved benefits for beneficiaries

Construction sector
Positive externatlities → Improved productivity / Improved capacity of contractors and TVET institutes to cooperate → Improved local workforce

TVET = technical and vocational education and training.
Source: Author.

3

PRINCIPLES OF INTEGRATING BUILD4SKILLS TRAINEESHIPS INTO ADB OPERATIONS

Cost-Efficient Integration into Project Processing, Procurement, and Implementation

The hallmark of Build4Skills is its innovative approach to processing and implementation. Traineeships are integrated into the regular project processing of infrastructure projects; it is not a separate technical assistance project or stand-alone activity. Through this integrative approach, traineeships are cost-efficient and easy to process.

Figure 5 compares the work effort (e.g., processing time, working hours) required for delivering traineeships as a stand-alone activity (left column) and traineeships integrated into infrastructure projects as promoted by Build4Skills (right column). Through the integration into already existing processes of infrastructure projects, some processes can be shortened or omitted. As a result, Build4Skills traineeships integrated into infrastructure projects are more cost-efficient than stand-alone traineeships (Figure 6).

This section summarizes how traineeships are seamlessly integrated into project processing and implementation and is described in further detail in the Build4Skills operational model (Chapter 4). The integration builds upon four practices by (i) aligning Build4Skills operational steps with the ADB project cycle, (ii) making traineeships a requirement in the procurement of civil works, (iii) delivering traineeships with contractors (public–private cooperation), and (iv) leveraging ADB-supported construction sites as traineeship sites.

Figure 5: Comparison of Work Effort Required for Delivering Traineeships as a Stand-Alone Activity vs. Being Integrated into Infrastructure Projects

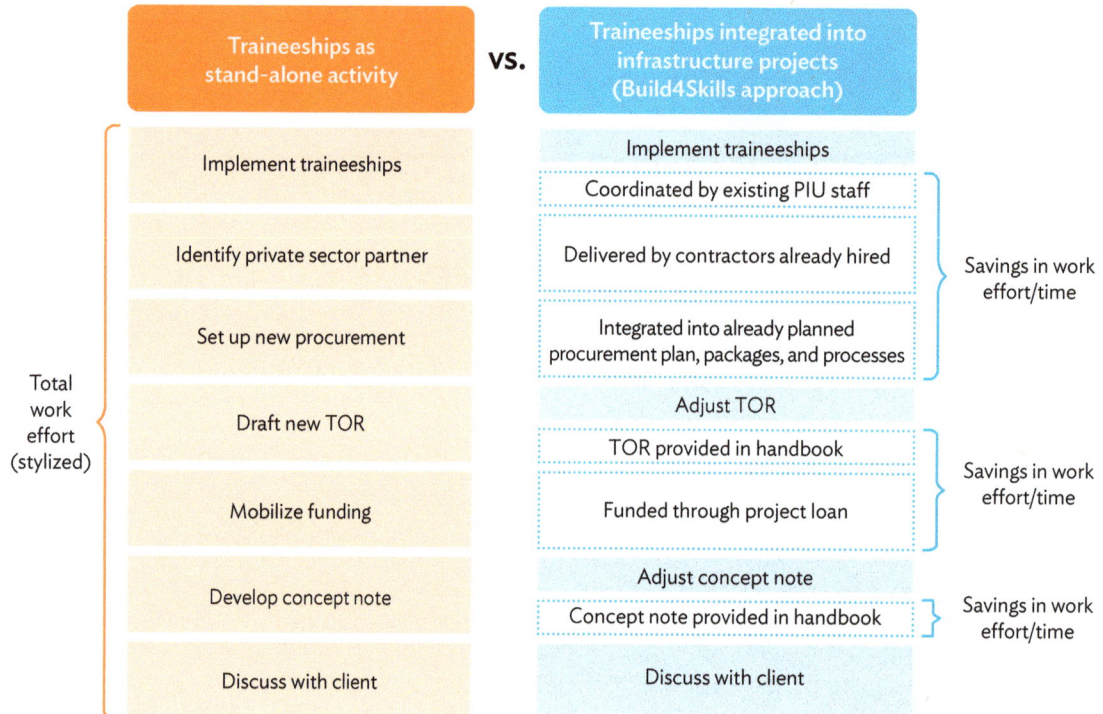

Traineeships as stand-alone activity	vs.	Traineeships integrated into infrastructure projects (Build4Skills approach)	
Implement traineeships		Implement traineeships	
		Coordinated by existing PIU staff	Savings in work effort/time
Identify private sector partner		Delivered by contractors already hired	
Set up new procurement		Integrated into already planned procurement plan, packages, and processes	
Draft new TOR		Adjust TOR	
		TOR provided in handbook	Savings in work effort/time
Mobilize funding		Funded through project loan	
Develop concept note		Adjust concept note	
		Concept note provided in handbook	Savings in work effort/time
Discuss with client		Discuss with client	

Total work effort (stylized)

PIU = project implementation unit, TOR = terms of reference.
Source: Author.

Figure 6: Four Ways Build4Skills Integrates into Infrastructure Projects

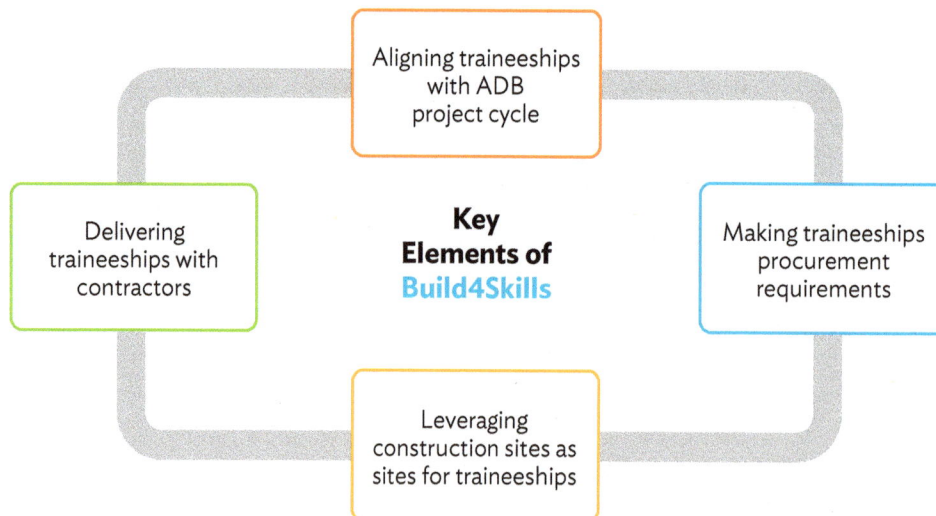

Aligning traineeships with ADB project cycle

Delivering traineeships with contractors

Key Elements of Build4Skills

Making traineeships procurement requirements

Leveraging construction sites as sites for traineeships

ADB = Asian Development Bank.
Source: Author.

1. Aligning Build4Skills Operational Model with the ADB Project Cycle

The handbook suggests implementing the Build4Skills traineeships in five stages (Figure 7) that are fully aligned with the ADB project cycle. This alignment means project teams process traineeships as part of regular project processing as shown in Figure 8.

Figure 7: Five Stages of the Build4Skills Operational Model

STAGE 1	STAGE 2	STAGE 3	STAGE 4	STAGE 5
Integrate Build4Skills into project design	Integrate Build4Skills requirements into procurement documents	Coordinate with contractors and schools	Deliver traineeships	Certify trainees and contractors

Source: Author.

Figure 8: How the Five Build4Skills Operational Stages Align with the ADB Project Cycle

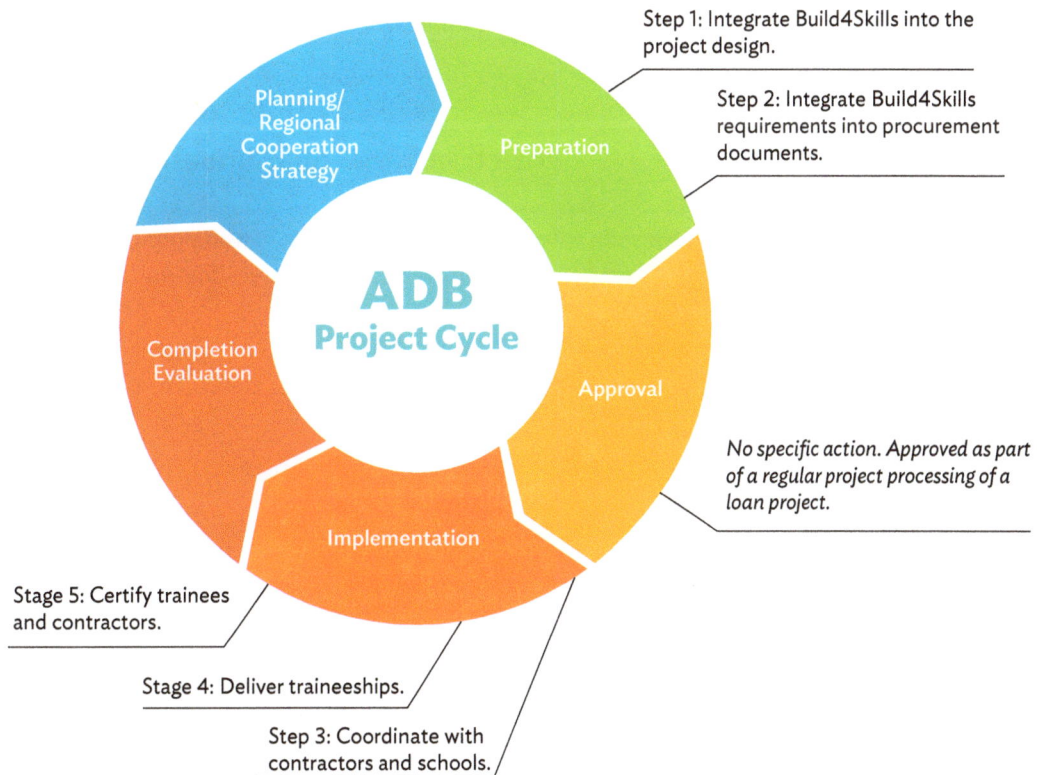

ADB Project Cycle

Planning/Regional Cooperation Strategy

Preparation

Step 1: Integrate Build4Skills into the project design.

Step 2: Integrate Build4Skills requirements into procurement documents.

Approval

No specific action. Approved as part of a regular project processing of a loan project.

Implementation

Step 3: Coordinate with contractors and schools.

Stage 4: Deliver traineeships.

Stage 5: Certify trainees and contractors.

Completion Evaluation

ADB = Asian Development Bank.
Source: Author, based on ADB project cycle.

Project teams follow Build4Skills stages 1 and 2 during the project preparation phase. This includes discussing and agreeing on the integration of traineeships into the project design with clients, and integrating traineeship requirements into civil work procurement and project documents. There is no specific Build4Skills stage at the approval phase as traineeships are approved as part of regular project documents. Stages 3, 4, and 5 happen during the project implementation phase. Traineeships are coordinated between contractors and the PIU and delivered on ADB-supported constructions sites. As long as the construction phase is ongoing, new traineeship batches can be arranged.

2. Making Traineeships Procurement Requirements in Civil Work Contract Packages

The second key practice to weave traineeships into the project designs of infrastructure projects is the integration of traineeship requirements into the procurement documents of selected civil work contract packages. OneADB teams only need to make minor additions to bidding documents during project preparation to incorporate traineeships in projects. The procurement steps are described in Chapter 4 and outlined in greater detail in the *Build4Skills Practice Guide for Procurement Practitioners*.

ADB's procurement guidance notes provide OneADB teams and the executing and/or implementing agencies with the basis to integrate social considerations into procurement:

(i)   ADB's *Strategic Procurement Planning*[10] outlines in step 4 of its guidance note how project teams can assess the potential of sustainable procurement in a project.

(ii) ADB's *Sustainable Public Procurement* (footnote 9) describes how social considerations can be integrated in procurement, including making traineeships a requirement and performance indicator in bidding documents.[11]

3. Leveraging ADB-Supported Construction Sites for Traineeships

The third practice for integrating traineeships into infrastructure projects is using project construction sites for traineeships. Construction sites are ideal for providing on-the-job traineeships and can be leveraged through civil work contract requirements.

Traineeships can be tailored to the context of the construction sector. Key parameters of traineeships that are typically part of traineeship contract specifications, are as follows:

(i)   **Location of training.** ADB-supported constructions sites.

(ii) **Duration.** 6–12 weeks, depending on the needs of contractors and availability of trainees.

(iii) **Trainees.** Enrolled TVET students, preferably seniors from local TVET institutes,[12] and/or recent TVET graduates (6 months or shorter).

---

[10]   ADB. 2021. *Strategic Procurement Planning: Guidance Note on Procurement.*

[11]   The example performance indicator suggested in the guidance note is stated as "10% of the total workforce on sites will be apprentices or trainees from the local vicinity."

[12]   A TVET institute can be a TVET school, polytechnic college, or a regular high school that offers a TVET track.

(iv) **Area of traineeship.** Any technical occupation as needed by contractors such as welders, electricians, concrete workers, or binders.

(v) **Trainers.** Staff of construction contractors.

(vi) **Frequency of traineeships.** Traineeships take place throughout the construction period, as per contractor needs and student availability.

4. Delivering Traineeships in Cooperation with Construction Contractors

The final key practice to integrate traineeships into ADB infrastructure projects is the delivery of traineeships directly through construction contractors.

Traineeships, by design, need to take place in a real-world environment and draw on industry know-how for effective technical training. Only contractors have the expertise and authority to deliver on-the-job training on construction sites. This is why delivery through contractors is critical and can be effectively ensured by making traineeships a procurement requirement.

Contractors are responsible for delivering traineeships on-site. They are expected to cooperate with local TVET institutes in the placement of TVET students as trainees. The PIU can connect contractors with TVET institutes and the youth. This public–private delivery arrangement is depicted in Figure 9 and can be formalized through cooperation agreements and traineeship contracts, which are outlined in this handbook. The main role of and benefits for the key stakeholders are summarized in Table 1.

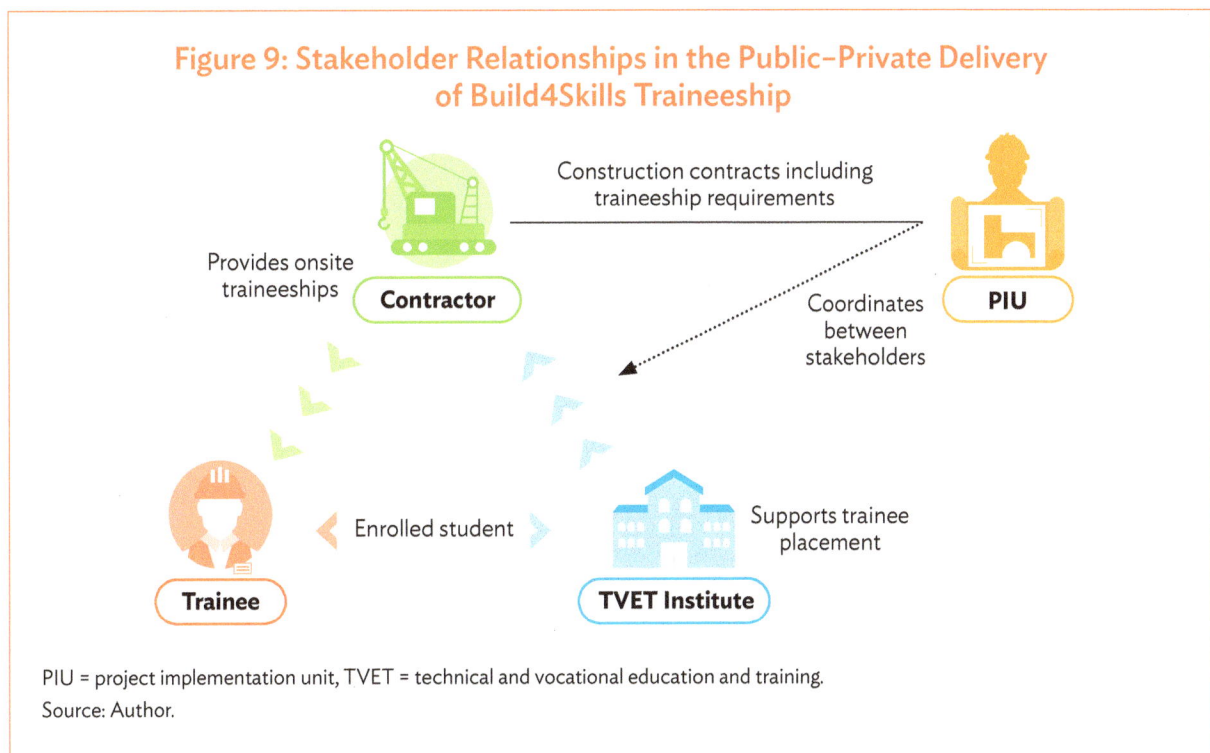

Figure 9: Stakeholder Relationships in the Public–Private Delivery of Build4Skills Traineeship

Provides onsite traineeships — **Contractor**

Construction contracts including traineeship requirements

PIU

Coordinates between stakeholders

Enrolled student

Trainee

Supports trainee placement

TVET Institute

PIU = project implementation unit, TVET = technical and vocational education and training.
Source: Author.

Table 1: Overview of Build4Skills Stakeholders' Roles and Benefits

Stakeholder	Main Role	Potential Benefits
Client (Executing Agency and/or Implementing Agency)	Agrees to integrate traineeships into project design. Sets traineeship requirements, targets and budget	• Additional social benefits for target community • Improved project reputation in the local community • Alignment of project with global best practices for quality/inclusive infrastructure • Improved quality of local workforce in the long term
Project implementation unit	Monitors traineeship implementation	
Contractor	Coordinates traineeships Delivers on-site traineeships	• Improved access to formally trained and hence, productive workers • Improved reputation in the local community • Improved competitiveness in future bids that assess the social track record of bidders
TVET institute	Makes students available	• Work-based training opportunities for its students • Improved capacity in cooperating with companies
Trainees	Participate in work-based training	• Improved technical and workplace skills • Improved employability for jobs

TVET = technical and vocational education and training.
Source: Author.

4

THE BUILD4SKILLS OPERATIONAL MODEL

This chapter is the main part of the handbook. It provides a step-by-step guide to processing and implementing traineeships as part of the ADB infrastructure projects. It describes how the five stages in the Build4Skills operational model can be implemented throughout the ADB project cycle following 15 steps (Figure 10) The following pages are organized along the three key phases of the ADB project cycle (i) project preparation, (ii) project approval, and (iii) project implementation. The Build4Skills five key stages and underlying 15 implementation steps are outlined throughout these phases as shown in Figure 10:

(i) **Stage 1** takes place during the initial project preparation and focuses on integrating traineeships into project design during project processing. The OneADB team, in dialogue with clients will:

1. discuss the integration of traineeships into the project with the client,
2. assess and document suitability in the strategic procurement planning report,
3. document and budget for traineeships in project documents,
4. brief project implementation unit on Build4Skills traineeships during the project inception mission.

(ii) **Stage 2** takes place at the advanced project preparation (procurement planning) and early implementation (tendering) phases. It focuses on making traineeship a procurement requirement in contract packages. It includes steps 5 and 6 and is implemented by the procurement consultants and specialists, who will:

5. integrate traineeship requirements into selected procurement contract packages,
6. tender for contracts and communicate with bidders.

(iii) **Stage 3** takes place at the project implementation phase and focuses on setting up traineeship arrangements. It includes steps 7–12 and is led by the contractor in cooperation with local TVET institutes. The contractor, in coordination with the PIU, will:

7. identify potential TVET partner institutes,
8. identify and share traineeship opportunities,
9. arrange instructor training for assigned contractor staff,
10. select TVET partner institute and sign of cooperation agreement,
11. select trainees and sign traineeship contracts,
12. complete quality checklist.

Figure 10: Build4Skills Operational Model Process Flow

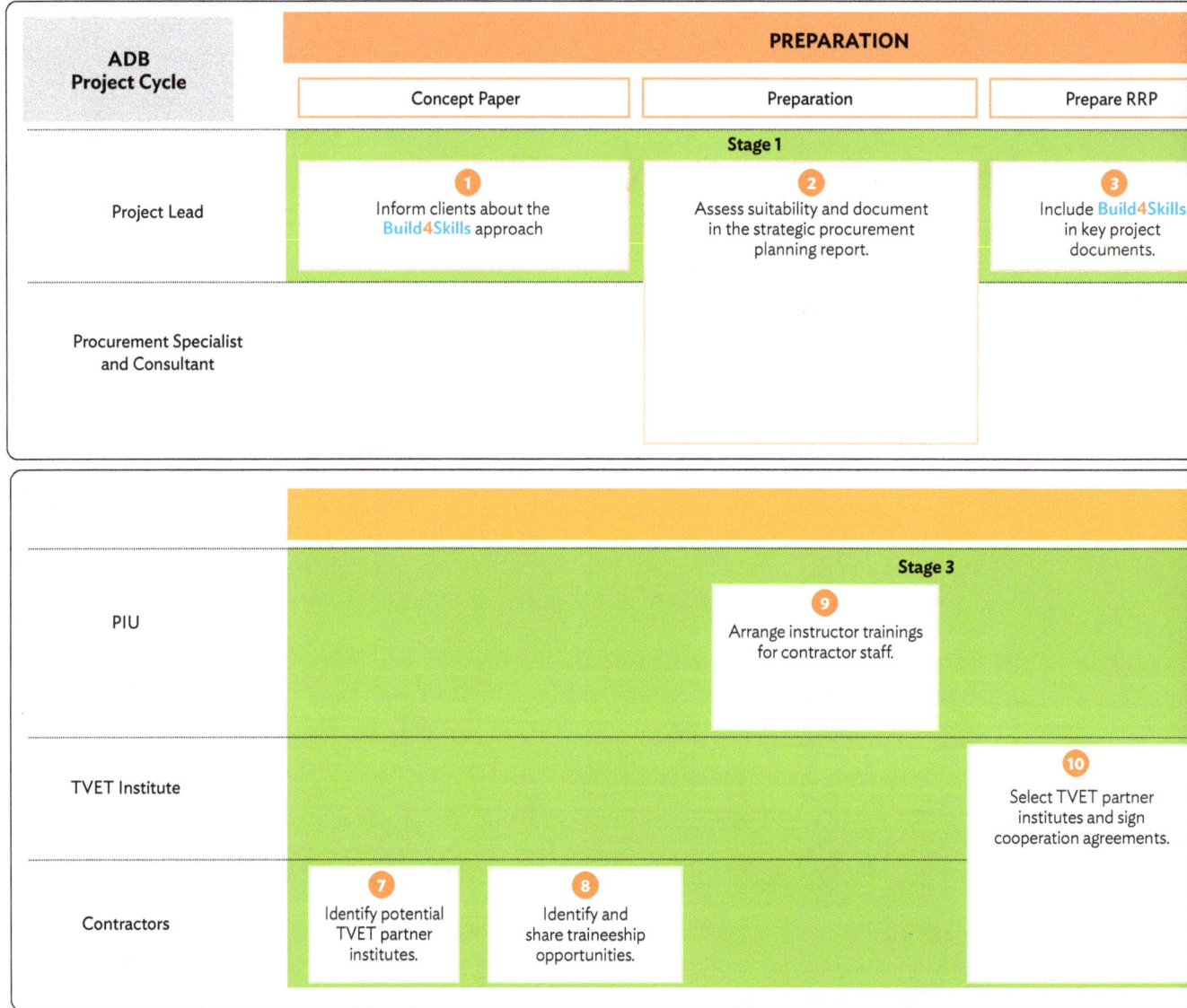

ADB Project Cycle	PREPARATION		
	Concept Paper	Preparation	Prepare RRP
	Stage 1		
Project Lead	**1** Inform clients about the Build4Skills approach	**2** Assess suitability and document in the strategic procurement planning report.	**3** Include Build4Skills in key project documents.
Procurement Specialist and Consultant			

			Stage 3
PIU			**9** Arrange instructor trainings for contractor staff.
TVET Institute			**10** Select TVET partner institutes and sign cooperation agreements.
Contractors	**7** Identify potential TVET partner institutes.	**8** Identify and share traineeship opportunities.	

ADB = Asian Development Bank, PIU = project implementation unit, RRP = report and recommendation of the President.

Notes: The blue bar on top represents the ADB project cycle to show when each Build4Skills step takes place in relation to project processing. Each row represents the area of responsibility of a stakeholder and indicates who is responsible for which step. The white numbered boxes represent each of the 15 steps to be implemented as described in the handbook.

Source: Author.

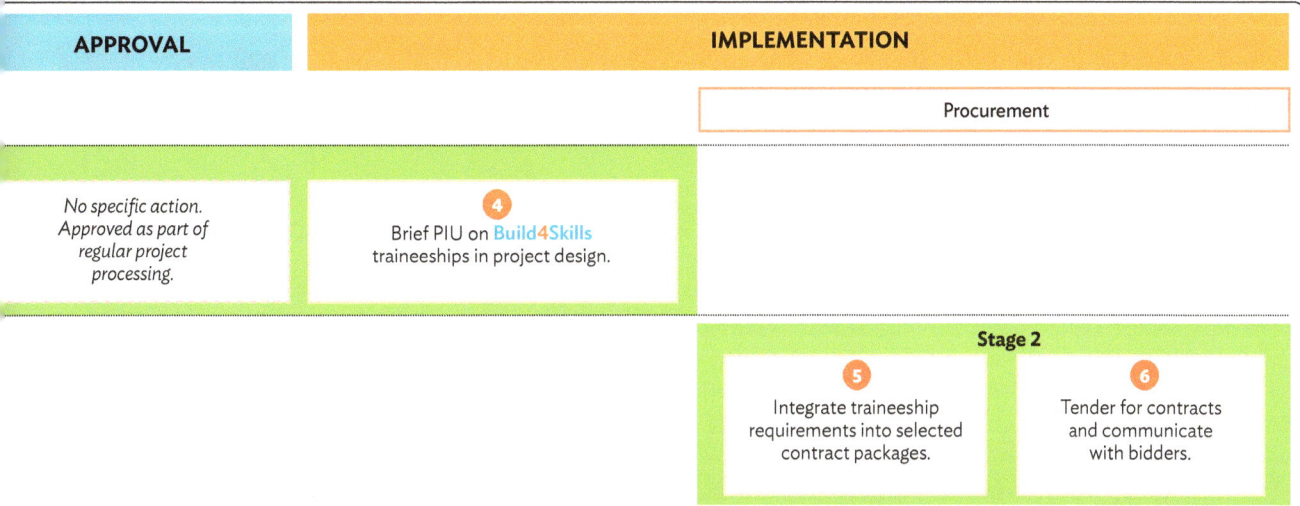

APPROVAL	IMPLEMENTATION		
		Procurement	
No specific action. Approved as part of regular project processing.	**4** Brief PIU on Build4Skills traineeships in project design.		
		Stage 2	
		5 Integrate traineeship requirements into selected contract packages.	**6** Tender for contracts and communicate with bidders.

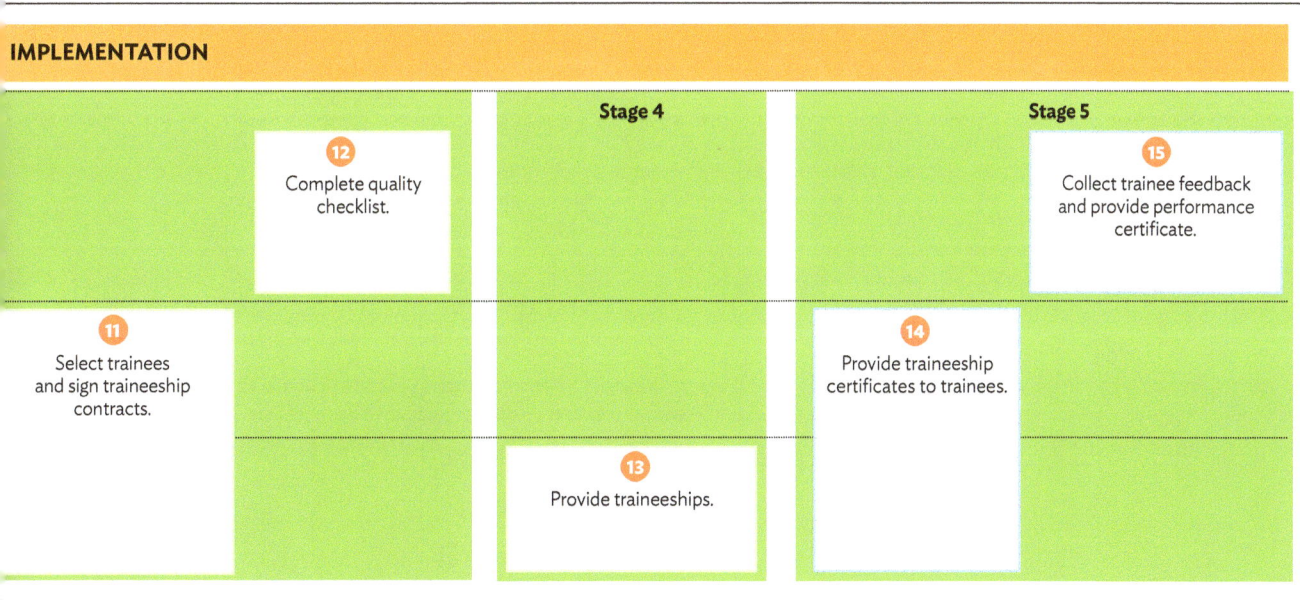

IMPLEMENTATION

		Stage 4	Stage 5
	12 Complete quality checklist.		**15** Collect trainee feedback and provide performance certificate.
11 Select trainees and sign traineeship contracts.			**14** Provide traineeship certificates to trainees.
		13 Provide traineeships.	

(iv) **Stage 4** takes place during project implementation and focuses on traineeship delivery. It includes step 13 and is implemented by contractors, who will:

13. provide traineeships.

(iv) **Stage 5** takes place during the project implementation phase and focuses on certifying trainees and contractors. It includes steps 14 and 15 and is coordinated by the PIU. The PIU, in coordination with the executing and implementing agencies, will:

14. provide traineeship certificate to trainees,
15. collect evidence, trainee feedback, and provide certificate of recognition to contractors.

Key success factors for processing and implementation teams are summarized in Box 2.

Box 2: Build4Skills Key Success Factors

For OneADB Processing Team	For Project Implementation Unit Team
✓ Inform clients about Build4Skills traineeships early on to get buy-in.	✓ Communicate roles and expectations clearly to contractors. They are willing partners when expectations are clear.
✓ Integrate Build4Skills traineeships in the strategic procurement and contract management plans.	✓ Proactively coordinate between contractors, TVET institutes, and trainees, so contractors can focus on their specialized role of providing on-the-job training.
✓ Include tasks on the monitoring and coordination of Build4Skills in the terms of reference of the project's construction supervision, procurement, and community engagement consultant.	✓ Recognize the achievements of contractors and the community throughout the implementation phase.
✓ Present the Build4Skills component to the PIU during the project inception mission.	✓ Consult the handbook for guidance and use the templates provided for quick implementation.
✓ Provide *Build4Skills Handbook* as well as the *Practice Guide for Procurement Practitioners* to PIU staff as a resource.	

PIU = project implementation unit, TVET = technical and vocational education and training.
Source: Author, based on feedback from projects.

PROJECT PREPARATION PHASE

STAGE 1: INTEGRATE BUILD4SKILLS TRAINEESHIPS INTO THE PROJECT DESIGN (STEPS 1–4)

Objective: In stage 1, the project team integrates Build4Skills traineeships into the project design and documents it as part of project processing. It includes steps 1–4 as outlined in Figure 11.

Figure 11: Timing of Steps 1-3 During the Project Preparation Phase

Project Preparation Phase			
Pre-Concept Paper	Concept Paper	Project Preparation	RRP Preparation
No specific Build4Skills actions required.	Discuss the integration of traineeships into the project with clients during consultation missions (step 1).	Assess suitability and document in strategic procurement planning report (step 2).	Record and budget for traineeships in project documents (step 3).

RRP = report and recommendation of the President.
Source: Author.

Ideally, project teams integrate Build4Skills traineeships in the project when drafting the project concept paper (Figure 11). It should be integrated before the report and recommendation of the President (RRP) is finalized and should include the following steps:

(i) **Pre-concept paper (optional).** The opportunity for traineeships is generally given on any construction site and does not require additional assessments.

(ii) **Concept paper.** Step 1 of the Build4Skills operational model may start when the concept paper is drafted. Clients are informed about the Build4Skills approach and would, ideally, agree to its integration into the project design.

(iii) **Project preparation.** In step 2, the project team assesses the suitability of Build4Skills for given civil works contract packages, and if found suitable, includes it in the strategic procurement planning (SPP).

(iv) **Preparation of the RRP.** In step 3, the project team records the approach in relevant project documents during the preparation of the RRP.

STEP 1	Discuss the Integration of Traineeships into the Project with the Client

At the end of step 1, the executing and/or implementing agency shall have agreed to include traineeships in the project design, which can be documented in the project concept paper.

Share Build4Skills concept note to inform clients about the Build4Skills traineeships. The executing agency's buy-in and ownership are highly important. Therefore, project leads should propose to clients the inclusion of traineeships in the project design during their first missions. The project lead shall provide the executing agency with the Build4Skills concept note (see Appendix). The concept note includes all relevant information about Build4Skills, including the rationale, benefits, delivery, stakeholder role, and funding. It can be adjusted to reflect the project-specific context and can be later attached to the project documents.

Discuss key messages about traineeships. In discussions with the client, the project lead may highlight key points about Build4Skills. These include how traineeships add value to the project, why implementation is feasible, and how costs are to be funded as detailed in Box 3.

Box 3: Key Messages for Clients About Build4Skills

Message 1: Traineeships add value to the project.

- Additional social impact: Traineeship opportunities improve youth employability and inclusion.
- Project reputation: The inclusion of youth improves the project's reputation in the local community.
- Alignment with best practices: The Build4Skills approach further aligns the project with the Asian Development Bank (ADB) Strategy 2030 and G20 Quality Infrastructure Investment Principles.[a]
- Contractor productivity: The cooperation with trainees and schools improves contractors' access to formally trained workers and therefore, productivity.

Message 2: Traineeships are easy to establish and implement.

- Clear approach: ADB provides project implementation units with a handbook, including templates, that details how traineeships can be efficiently set up.
- Low administrative work: The approach is integrated in regular project processing, and the scope is small and thus manageable for the project implementation unit.
- Flexible procurement: Procurement officers and consultants can integrate traineeships as either a mandatory or voluntary, competitive or noncompetitive requirement, keeping in line with ADB and national procurement regulations.

Message 3: Traineeships are low cost and can be funded through a marginal increase in the loan.

- Traineeship costs are kept marginal in relation to the total investment volume. Clients can set a traineeship budget by either setting first a traineeship target and deriving costs from it, or, alternatively, by earmarking a traineeship budget, which is recommended to be between 0.25%–0.5% of the estimated contract price for civil work contract packages (CWCPs) that incorporate traineeships.
- Optionally, for every year of construction, $1,500 may be added to the training budget for each CWCP that applies the Build4Skills approach to fund capacity training for contractors.

[a] ADB. 2018. *Strategy 2030: Achieving a Prosperous, Inclusive, Resilient, and Sustainable Asia and the Pacific*. Manila; *G20 Principles for Quality Infrastructure Investment*.
Source: Author.

Document integration into project design in aide memoire and project concept note. Once the client agrees to include traineeships in the project, the project lead may document the integration of the Build4Skills approach in the aide memoire, memorandum of understanding, and/or project concept note. The project lead may also inform the internal ADB team, including safeguard and procurement specialists, about the consideration of Build4Skills in the project design in anticipation of upcoming processing steps.

STEP 2   Assess and Document Suitability in the Strategic Procurement Planning Report

At the end of step 2, the OneADB team shall have identified all contract packages in which traineeships can be integrated.

After the client has agreed to integrate traineeships into the project in step 1, the project team moves to step 2, which overlaps with the SPP of a given project.

Identify suitable civil works contract packages. During the SPP, the OneADB team, including the ADB procurement and safeguard specialists, and the implementing agency identify the civil work contract packages in the procurement plan that are suitable for integrating traineeships. The suitability is determined by three criteria: minimum civil work contract package price, minimum duration of a given contract package, and proximity to TVET institute (Table 2). Civil work contract packages are assessed separately.

Table 2: Criteria to Determine Build4Skills Suitability of Civil Works Contract Packages

Suitability Criteria	Suitable	Not Suitable
The construction duration is longer than 12 months.	Yes	No
The contract price of individual civil work contract package is greater than $500,000.	Yes	No
The construction site is located 30 miles or less from relevant TVET institutes. (If unknown, this criterion can be skipped.)	Yes, or unknown	No
	Contract package is suitable, proceed	**Contract package is not suitable**

TVET = technical and vocational education and training.
Source: Author.

The first two suitability criteria can be determined by checking the project procurement plan. As for the third criterion (proximity of TVET institutes), it can be assumed that in urban areas, TVET institutes are located near construction sites. In rural areas, the choice and availability of institutes shall be discussed with the client. If the distance between the construction site and TVET institutes cannot be estimated at this stage, Build4Skills is still considered suitable and shall proceed.

Document suitable contract packages in strategic procurement planning report. The OneADB team records the suitable contract packages in the sustainable procurement and packaging sections of the SPP report.

Document and Set Budget for Traineeships in Project Documents

At the end of step 3, Build4Skills traineeships shall have been incorporated in project documents.

After the client's confirmation (step 1) and the identification of suitable contract packages (step 2), the project team records the integration of traineeships into project documents (Table 3).

Record Build4Skills in project documents. Table 3 outlines how OneADB project processing teams and consultants can document the integration of traineeships into project documents, including in the project administration manual, the RRP, contribution to corporate results framework, and bidding documents. The Build4Skills concept note that was shared with clients in step 1 shall also be added to the project documents.

Table 3: How to Integrate Traineeships into Project Documents

Project Document	Actions for Project Teams	Check
PAM	In the procurement and consulting service section of the PAM, add text that Build4Skills traineeships are incorporated into civil work contracts:	
	"The procurement approach includes the incorporation of skilled traineeship opportunities in civil works contract. The traineeships will be designed in accordance with ADB's *Build4Skills Handbook* and its associated practice guide [insert footnote references]. Contract specifications will include detailed requirements for the design and delivery of the traineeships with a target of XX traineeships being delivered through the Project."	
	In the procurement plan, adjust the estimated values of selected contract packages that will integrate Build4Skills traineeships to reflect the traineeship budget (see Box 4).	
	In the TOR of construction supervision consultant, national procurement specialist, project director, and civil work coordinator, add this responsibility:	
	"Monitor and coordinate Build4Skills activities with contractors, in consideration of ADB's *Build4Skills Handbook* and the *Practice Guide for Procurement Practitioners*, including but not limited to, incorporating traineeships requirements into bidding documents, reviewing contractors' traineeship plans and progress reports, verifying evidence for delivery of traineeships according to specifications, collecting trainee feedback."	
Build4Skills concept note	Attach the Build4Skills concept note as a linked document to the project documents (see template in Appendix).	
Contribution to corporate results framework	Tag relevant indicators in the contribution to ADB Strategy 2030 operational priorities project document. Relevant result and tracking indicators are 1.1(.1), 1.2(.3), 2.2(.1), and 6.1(.2) (Appendix).	
RRP	State in the RRP that Build4Skills traineeships are integrated into the project. If necessary, add to supplementary Appendix.	
Contract Packages (see also step 5)	Integrate traineeship requirements into procurement documents as outlined in step 5 of the handbook and elaborated in detail in the *Practice Guide for Procurement Practitioners*.	
	Adjust the bill of quantities of the selected contract packages to reflect the Build4Skills traineeship budget as outlined in detail in the *Practice Guide for Procurement Practitioners* (see Box 4).	

ADB = Asian Development Bank, PAM = project administration manual, RRP = report and recommendation of the President, TOR = terms of reference, TVET = technical and vocational education and training.
Source: Author.

Box 4: How to Budget for Traineeships for the Bill of Quantities

OneADB teams may follow one of two approaches in setting a traineeships budget to be included in the bill of quantities. Either the client sets a feasible traineeship target, and costs are estimated based on the target, or, alternatively, the client earmarks a traineeship budget which is recommended to between 0.25%–0.5% (depending on loan volume) of the value of each civil work contract package that includes traineeship requirements. The *Build4Skills Practice Guide for Procurement Practitioners* outlines both approaches in greater detail. The traineeship budget is to cover trainee allowance, insurance, and personal protective equipment.

ADB = Asian Development Bank.
Source: Author.

PROJECT APPROVAL PHASE

There are no specific actions in this phase as Build4Skills traineeships are integrated into regular project documents (step 3) and await approval as part of regular project processing.

PROJECT IMPLEMENTATION PHASE

After the approval of the infrastructure project, the main responsibility for project implementation, including procurement, moves to the PIU. The handover of Build4Skills activities is facilitated during the project inception mission.

STEP 4   Brief Project Implementation Unit on Build4Skills Traineeships During the Project Inception Mission.

Present Build4Skills traineeship component to PIU. OneADB teams should include Build4Skills in the agenda of the inception mission to inform the PIU about its further implementation. The team shall present the Build4Skills concept once more, highlight the identified suitable civil work contract packages, outline the general procurement approach, and point out PIU staff whose terms of reference include responsibilities for coordinating traineeships, as recommended in step 3.

Ask PIU to nominate a Build4Skills focal point. The OneADB team should request the PIU to assign a formal focal point—ideally someone from the managerial level QWII—for Build4Skills activities, which shall be recorded in the mission's aide-mémoire.

Share *Build4Skills Handbook* with PIU. The project team shall share the *Build4Skills Handbook* and the *Practice Guide for Procurement Practitioners* with the PIU as a resource for implementation. The team should highlight that steps 5–15 of the handbook aim to guide PIU staff in coordinating traineeships with contractors and include templates for ease of use. The PIU shall use the steps as an orientation but may also implement it differently to suit their context.

Brief the procurement consultants. The procurement consultants play a central role in the immediate steps after the inception mission (steps 5 and 6), as well as in contract management throughout the construction phase. The OneADB team shall therefore clearly inform the consultants about their role in incorporating Build4Skills requirements in the identified civil works contract packages and contract management plan. In the briefing, the OneADB team may (i) highlight the consultants' key responsibilities (Table 4) and (ii) share the *Build4Skills Practice Guide for Procurement Practitioners.*

Table 4: Key Responsibilities of Procurement Consultants

Activity	Key Responsibilities
Procurement of Build4Skills traineeships	<ul><li>Follow strategic procurement plan.</li><li>Integrate traineeships requirements into suitable contract packages.</li><li>Adjust bill of quantities of contract packages as needed.</li><li>Incorporate traineeship requirements into the contract management plan.</li><li>Address questions of bidders.</li></ul>
Contract management implementation	<ul><li>Track contractors' reporting on traineeships.</li><li>Verify the provision of traineeships by requesting proof of traineeships (traineeship contracts) and trainee feedback evaluation results.</li><li>Coordinate collection of trainee feedback.</li><li>Assess contractors' traineeship performance and provide certificate.</li><li>Manage payments related to traineeships.</li><li>Manage claims and disputes, e.g., regarding occupational health and safety issues, trainee stipend payments, or poor trainee feedback.</li></ul>

Source: Author.

STAGE 2: INTEGRATE TRAINEESHIP REQUIREMENTS INTO PROCUREMENT AND CONTRACT DOCUMENTS (STEPS 5 AND 6)

Objective. In stage 2, procurement consultants, with the support of the ADB procurement specialist, integrate traineeship requirements into procurement documents and finalize the award of contract. It includes steps 5 and 6.

STEP 5   Integrate Traineeship Requirements into Selected Procurement Contract Packages

At the end of step 5, Build4Skills traineeships shall have been integrated into procurement documents and the provisional budgets updated accordingly.

Follow the Build4Skills Practice Guide for Procurement Practitioners. The client with support of the procurement consultant and the OneADB team incorporates traineeship requirements into the procurement documents of each civil work contract package identified as suitable in the SPP report (step 2). How traineeship requirements are to be incorporated into bidding documents is explained in greater technical detail in the supplementary *Build4Skills Practice Guide for Procurement Practitioners.* The practice guide provides template traineeship requirements that can be directly transferred into bidding documents. It also outlines how to calculate the provisional sum for traineeships to be included in the bill of quantities. It is specifically aimed at procurement specialists and consultants. Key points of the procurement approach as outlined in the practice guide include:

- Traineeship requirements are incorporated in the contract specification requirements of bidding documents.
- A provisional sum for traineeship is included in the bill of quantities or pricing schedule as a fixed cost.
- A traineeship target is included in the bill of quantities.
- The traineeship requirements, target, and budget are the same for all bidders.
- Technical proposals by bidders are optional to reduce bidding workload.
- There are two approaches to calculating the provisional sum and setting a traineeship target.
- The provided traineeship requirements and specifications template may be adjusted to reflect local circumstances.

STEP 6   Tender for Contracts and Communicate with Bidders

At the end of step 6, the contract shall have been awarded.

After the integration of traineeship into procurement documents and the project's official approval, the procurement consultants and staff of the PIU start the tendering process.

Share frequently asked questions with bidders. During the tendering process, bidders may have questions regarding traineeship requirements. The implementing agency or the PIU can share a frequently asked question (FAQ) guide to provide more details. An exemplary FAQ, which answers questions around the nature and implementation of traineeships, is provided in the Appendix. The FAQs can be adjusted to reflect context-specific information.

Communicate with bidders. In the exchange with bidders (e.g., at a pre-bidding meeting), the PIU shall note and communicate the following points to reassure the feasibility of a traineeship:

(i) **It is feasible.** The contractors' main task is to provide on-the-job training in work areas that are well-known to them. The incremental overhead is expected to be minimal and can be readily absorbed by the contractor.

(ii) **It is aligned with industry hiring practices.** Traineeships last 6–12 weeks, matching the construction industry's short-term hiring practices. They do not result in long-term commitments.

(iii) **It incurs no direct costs.** Costs related to traineeships are typically priced into the loan and thus do not create a financial burden [verify with given project design].

(iv) **It is not a new practice.** Most companies have experience with staff training such as onboarding, occupational health and safety, new equipment, etc.

(v) **Contractors can benefit from traineeships.** These benefits include (a) having an improved access to formally trained and productive workers, (b) saving costs by working with local human resources, (c) improving the company's reputation, and (d) improving competitiveness for future bids that assess the social track record of bidders.

Incorporate traineeship requirements into the contract management plan. At the pre-contract award stage, Build4Skills traineeship requirements shall be included in the contract management plan following ADB's *Contract Management: Guidance Note on Procurement*.[13] This will ensure that the requirements are monitored, and potential shortcomings are addressed through corrective actions.

The Build4Skills stage 2 ends with the award of contract to the winning bidder.

STAGE 3: COORDINATE TRAINEESHIP ARRANGEMENTS WITH CONTRACTORS AND TECHNICAL AND VOCATIONAL EDUCATION AND TRAINING INSTITUTES

Objective. Following the successful award of contract, the Build4Skills operational model moves to stage 3. The objective of the stage is for the PIU to ensure that the contractor makes all necessary preparations and successfully sets up traineeships in cooperation with TVET institutes.

Key milestones of stage 3 for the PIU. In stage 3, the contractor in coordination with the PIU is responsible for achieving three key milestones before traineeships can go ahead. Contractors need to have (i) identified traineeship opportunities and partner TVET institutes (steps 7–9), (ii) formalized partnerships between contractors and TVET institutes (step 10), and (iii) signed traineeship contracts with trainees (step 11). The PIU confirms the completion of all these steps by completing a quality checklist for quality backstopping (steps 12). A summary of milestones is presented in Figure 12.

Figure 12: Key Milestones of Stage 3

Steps	Steps 7–9	Step 10	Steps 11 and 12
Milestones	Traineeship opportunities and TVET institutes identified	Partnerships between contractors and TVET institutes are formalized	Traineeship contracts are signed, and quality checklist completed
Key activities performed by PIU at stage 3	• Inform local TVET institutes about traineeships. • Request contractors to provide information about traineeship opportunities. • Arrange training for contractor staff.	• Select TVET institute providing relevant trainings. • Coordinate signing of cooperation agreement between TVET institutes and contractors.	• Facilitate selection of trainees with TVET institutes and contractors. • Coordinate drafting of traineeship contracts ensuring decent and safe traineeship conditions. • Complete quality checklist.

PIU = project implementation unit, TVET = technical and vocational education and training.
Source: Author.

---

[13]   ADB. 2021. *Contract Management: Guidance Note on Procurement*.

Cooperation agreements and traineeship contracts. Key documents used in stage 3 are cooperation agreements and traineeship contracts. To structure the cooperation between stakeholders, contractors and TVET institutes should sign cooperation agreements, and contractors and trainees should sign traineeship contracts. Such agreements (see templates provided in the Appendix) are common in traineeship arrangements. The purpose of each document is highlighted in Table 5.

Table 5: Difference Between Cooperation Agreements and Traineeship Contracts

Item	Purpose
Cooperation agreement	This agreement between contractors and TVET institutes confirms the mutual intention to cooperate, which creates plannability. It may outline traineeship conditions but does not include details about traineeship terms and conditions.
Traineeship contract	This contract between trainees, contractors, and TVET institutes outlines the specific terms and conditions of traineeships, such as working hours and provision of stipends. Each trainee signs a traineeship contract.

TVET = technical and vocational education and training.
Source: Author.

The PIU will go through stage 3 multiple times. The PIU may go through stage 3, and consequently, stages 4 and 5, more than once as traineeships may be organized in batches throughout the construction period. This is because construction sites can only offer a limited number of traineeships at a time. Different skills sets—and therefore different trainees—may be needed at different points of the construction. Traineeships can be reliably planned for 6–12 months in advance, a workable planning horizon for contractors and TVET institutes. Box 5 highlights the three approaches the PIU may take to effectively cooperate with contractors.

Box 5: How the Project Implementation Unit Can Engage Contractors to Be Active and Responsive

- Coordinate proactively. The project implementation unit (PIU) may proactively coordinate traineeships with technical and vocational education and training (TVET) institutes and contractors, instead of waiting for contractors to become active. This can mean requesting specific information about upcoming traineeship opportunities (see step 8) and setting up meetings between contractors and local TVET schools to initiate dialogue (see step 10).

- Track progress. The PIU regularly inquires with contractors about progress to show that responsibilities are tracked, and results are expected. Contractors are requested to submit progress reports.

- Certify performance. At the end of the project, the PIU provides contractors with a Build4Skills certificate of recognition (see stage 5 for details on contractor performance assessment).

Source: Author.

STEP 7   Identify Potential TVET Partner Institutes

At the end of step 7, local TVET institutes shall have been identified and informed about Build4Skills traineeship opportunities.

The objective of step 7 is to identify relevant training providers and inform them about the upcoming traineeship opportunities. The final TVET partner institute will be selected later in step 9, when more information on traineeship opportunities is available.

Identify TVET institutes. The contractor identifies TVET institutes that offer training programs in construction-related professions that match the needs of the project's construction site (see step 8) and are, ideally, located near it. Alternatively, the PIU may proactively suggest suitable TVET institutes to contractors. The PIU may request the project's implementation partners, local government units, education authorities, or international donors to assist in identifying relevant local TVET institutes.

Inform TVET institutes about traineeships. Once potential partner TVET institutes have been identified, the contractor shall contact their management (e.g., school principal) about the Build4Skills initiative. The PIU may support the contractor in (i) sharing an information sheet with TVET institutes that summarizes the traineeship initiative (see template in the Appendix); and (ii) requesting from them general information such as the institute's qualification programs, previous experience with work-based training (WBT), and interest in the cooperation.

STEP 8   Identify and Share Traineeship Opportunities

At the end of step 8, the PIU shall have identified contractors' demand for trainees for the next 6–12 months.

Request contractors to provide traineeship opportunities. Concurrent with step 7, contractors need to provide an overview of the upcoming traineeship opportunities on their construction sites in the coming 6–12 months. This overview may be shared with potential partner TVET institutes.

Share the request for trainees' form. Upcoming opportunities can be collected through a request for trainees' form (see template in the Appendix) that the PIU shares with contractors or, alternatively, the contractor may provide a high level traineeship plan. It is important that contractors provide sufficient details about upcoming traineeship opportunities to identify suitable partner TVET institutes and students (Box 6).

Box 6: Why the Information in the Request for Trainees' Form Is Important

The request for trainees includes information that the project implementation unit (PIU) requires to implement next steps:

- **Occupational areas of traineeships.** This is needed so that the contractor can identify the technical and vocational education and training (TVET) institutes that offer training programs in areas that match requested traineeships. The PIU shall deny any contractor requests for unskilled roles such as helper or manual laborer.

- **Possible dates of traineeships.** This allows TVET institutes to plan and verify if their students are available on the proposed dates.

- **Number of traineeships.** This allows TVET institutes to verify if they can provide the required number of students, or if additional TVET institutes must be tapped to meet the requirement.

- **Location of traineeships.** This is needed to verify that the distance between TVET institutes and the proposed construction sites is feasible for students.

Source: Author.

STEP 9   Arrange Instructor Training for Assigned Contractor Staff

At the end of step 9, company instructors shall have participated in training. Depending on the availability of contractor staff, this step can also occur at a later point in time, concurrent with steps 10 and 11.

Contractors assign staff as trainee instructors. In preparation for the traineeships, the PIU focal point requests contractors to assign staff members as trainee instructors. These instructors are tasked to supervise trainees during the traineeship and to act as the PIU's contact persons. Several staff members can be nominated by contractors. The role of instructors is essential to ensure that trainees become productive quickly and work safely.

Arrange instructor training for assigned contractor staff. If the project has allocated a budget for the training of contractors, the PIU shall arrange instructor training for staff assigned as instructors. Such training is recommended to ensure the quality and safety of traineeships and the capacity development of contractors. Instructor training covers pedagogy and occupational health and safety.

Pedagogy training typically includes four core skills: identifying learning goals, developing a learning plan, teaching practically on the job, and providing feedback. These skills can be learned through short-term training (2–14 days), and any course that touches upon these four areas is suitable for instructor training. A useful reference point is the *Ausbildung der Ausbilder* (AdA) certificate, which is the international standard provided by business chambers in Asia. Other training institutes or business associations may offer similar courses.

It is good practice for all instructors to also undertake occupational and health safety orientation as this helps them ensure a safe work environment for staff as well as trainees. Recommended trainings include ADB's Health, Safety & Security online course and Mental Health and Wellbeing in the Workplace online courses, which can be accessed on ADB's e-learning platform.

STEP 10   Select Technical and Vocational Education and Training Partner Institute and Sign Cooperation Agreement

At the end of step 10, selected TVET institutes and contractors shall have signed cooperation agreements.

Select a TVET institute. In step 7, TVET institutes were identified. In step 10, the contractor selects a suitable TVET partner institute that provides training programs in the traineeship areas requested by the contractor in step 8.

Coordinate the signing of a cooperation agreement between contractors and TVET institutes. After the selection, the PIU may inquire if contractors have signed cooperation agreement (see Appendix) with TVET institutes. While not strictly needed for the delivery of traineeships, the agreement is important as it creates certainty about the intention to arrange traineeships, instead of just having an informal commitment. The PIU may support the contractor by sharing the cooperation agreement template provided in the Appendix with them. Changes to the agreement template may be made to reflect context-specific circumstances.

The purpose of the cooperation agreement is to document the intent of cooperation between contractors and TVET institutes. They outline the key responsibilities of each party to ensure they are clear about their future roles. It may, for example, indicate prospective dates for traineeships (e.g., construction season, alignment with school timetable) as well as prospective duration (6–12 weeks); work and training areas; and traineeship locations. By outlining a general direction, contractors and TVET institutes can plan for traineeships. The agreement does not need to include all details of traineeship terms and conditions as these are finalized in step 11, during the signing of traineeship contracts between contractors and trainees.

STEP 11   Select Trainees and Sign Traineeship Contracts

At the end of step 11, students shall have been selected, and contractors shall have signed traineeship contracts with trainees and their TVET institute. The various tasks of step 11 are summarized in Figure 13.

Figure 13: Key Tasks to Be Implemented in Step 11

| Share information about traineeships opportunities with TVET institutes and request to nominate students. | TVET institutes select students for traineeships in coordination with contractors. | Request contractors to sign traineeship contracts with selected students and their TVET institutes. | Support drafting contracts if needed and verify that drafts include stipulations for decent and safe traineeship conditions. | Contractors sign traineeship contracts with trainees and their TVET institute. |

TVET = technical and vocational education and training.
Source: Author.

Contractors share traineeship opportunities and selection criteria with TVET institutes. The contractor informs the selected TVET institutes about upcoming traineeship opportunities on the given construction site. As an option, the PIU may also be included in the communication with TVET institutes. The contractor may ask TVET institutes to assist in shortlisting suitable students for selection. Contractors can freely set criteria for shortlisting and selecting trainees. Trainees should at minimum be enrolled in qualifications that match traineeship requirements. In addition, it is recommended to instruct TVET institutes to assist in shortlisting students who are mature and have strong social skills—consequently, senior students and recent graduates may be preferred. Other possible shortlisting criteria may include (i) a minimum age (typical age range between 16 and 22 years), (ii) minimum level of grades/score, (iii) language skills, and/or (iv) minimum level of qualification achieved. Finally, equal opportunities for men and women should be ensured.

Shortlist and select trainees. TVET institutes shall promote traineeship opportunities among its students. The PIU and the contractor shall encourage TVET institutes to promote traineeships among female students where appropriate. It is best practice to shortlist and select trainees together with contractors. The selection arrangement can be discussed during the cooperation agreement in step 11. However, joint selection is optional as contractors may not want to spend time on the selection process. The TVET institute may provide contractors with a list of shortlisted students. The contractor should ensure that the list includes key information such as students' names, age, qualification background, gender, contact details, as well as languages and academic scores.

Draft traineeship contracts. After students have been selected, the contractor shall sign traineeship contracts with students (or if underage, with their legal guardians). The PIU may support contractors in drafting traineeship contracts, as well as terms and conditions, by taking the traineeship contract template in the Appendix as a starting point.

The PIU can also set up a structured discussion between stakeholders using the meeting agenda provided in the Appendix. The agenda lists many of the crucial topics that should be discussed in a traineeship contract.

Make the traineeship contract template context-specific. The form and context of traineeship contracts can differ from country to country. The traineeship agreement template provided in the Appendix is a general example that may be adjusted to reflect country specifics and laws. Given the short duration, the focus on training, and the provision of a stipend (not salary), Build4Skills traineeships resemble internship arrangements rather than employment; the difference can affect the legal form and content of contracts (Box 7). The PIU may consult with its human resource specialists, contractors, and TVET institutes about labor and TVET laws.

Signing of traineeship contracts. At the end of step 11, each trainee (or if required, their legal guardian) shall have signed a traineeship contract with the contractor and TVET institutes. All signatories shall receive a copy of the contract.

Box 7: Considerations when Drafting Traineeship Contracts

A traineeship contract is an agreement between the contractor, trainees (or their legal guardians), and the technical and vocational education and training (TVET) institute that lays down the specific conditions of the traineeship. This may have to be aligned with labor or TVET laws, depending on how far national laws regulate this kind of training arrangement.

Traineeships are commonly conceived as either an employment, apprenticeship, or internship contract. For employment, the relationship between the company and trainee is defined by the remuneration for productive labor, and the trainee tends to be regarded as an employee. For internship, the relationship is defined by training, tends to be short term, and the trainee is regarded as a student, not an employee. In this arrangement, trainees might receive a stipend but not a salary. For apprenticeship, those that last 6 months or less tend to resemble internship arrangements, while those that are long term tend to resemble employment arrangements. Depending on the arrangement, different laws and regulation may apply.

Source: Author.

STEP 12   Complete Quality Checklist

At the end of step 12, the PIU shall have checked and confirmed all points in the checklist.

Go through the checklist. Before the start of traineeships, the PIU shall go through the Build4Skills checklist (Table 6) to ensure that all important preparatory issues have been addressed by contractors. The *Build4Skills Practice Guide for Procurement Practitioners* recommends making traineeship related disbursements dependent on the successful completion of the checklist to incentivize contractors to properly set up traineeships in particular with regard to occupational health and safety (Box 8). The checklist may be amended in case additional responsibilities or safeguard considerations are identified for the given context. Traineeships shall not proceed until all points in the checklist have been satisfactorily addressed.

Table 6: Build4Skills Quality Checklist

Quality Criteria	Check
Traineeship contracts have been signed by all stakeholders including students or their legal guardians.	
All trainees have received occupational health and safety training, which is also documented (e.g., participants list).	
All trainees have personal protective equipment as required for the construction site.	
All trainees have accident insurance for the traineeship period.	
Contractors have assigned an on-site instructor for the trainees.	
The terms of how and when trainees receive their stipends are clear.	
Trainees have been fully briefed about the traineeships, their responsibilities, and organizational issues.	
Transport and food provisions for trainees have been considered and addressed.	
For female trainees, considerations for a gender-sensitive traineeship environment have been made.	
For underage trainees, appropriate considerations and measures have been made.	

Source: Author.

Completing the checklist is critical. The importance of supervision and health and safety of trainees is highlighted by the International Labour Organization Convention No. 138 on Minimum Age and Convention No. 182 on Child Labour.[14] Both conventions point out that the provision of adequate training, protection, and supervision at the traineeship place is a prerequisite for providing on-the-job training to youth.

Box 8: Occupational Health and Safety Training

Trainees shall receive adequate occupational health and safety (OHS) training under the guidance of contractors who are familiar with industry standards, contractual requirements, and the context of the construction sites. The training shall include formal OHS training complemented by a site-specific safety orientation. The completion of the trainings should be documented for each trainee.

In some contexts, appropriate OHS training may be readily available. It is recommended to consider providing the Asian Development Bank's Health, Safety & Security course and Mental Health and Wellbeing in the Workplace course available online.

Source: Author.

STAGE 4: DELIVER TRAINEESHIPS

Objective: Contractors deliver on-site traineeships.

In stage 4, all preparatory work has been completed, and contractors are now in the lead to provide youth with traineeships on construction sites.

STEP 13   Contractors Provide Traineeships

At the end of step 13, contractors shall have started to deliver traineeships.

Contractor provides traineeships. The contractors, with the assigned instructor in the lead, supervise trainees and provide on-the-job training in line with traineeship contract specifications.

Trainees may document their training or work in a traineeship journal, which can serve as a basis to recognize the traineeship as part of students' qualification program. It is the TVET institute's responsibility to support trainees in this regard and to inform contractors.

The PIU and TVET institutes check in on trainees. The PIU, in coordination with TVET institutes, shall occasionally follow up with trainees during their traineeship to ensure that contracts are fully implemented, and trainees have a safe and decent working environment.

---

[14] International Labour Organization. 1973. Minimum Age Convention, 1973 (No. 138); ILO. 1999. Worst Forms of Child Labour Convention, 1999 (No. 182).

STAGE 5: CERTIFY TRAINEES AND CONTRACTORS

Objective. The contractor certifies trainees and starts planning for the next traineeship batch while the project is active. At the end of construction contracts, the PIU provides a traineeship certificate of recognition to contractors.

After each traineeship batch, the PIU leads in undertaking wrap-up activities and recognizing the commitment of all stakeholders.

STEP 14   Provide Traineeship Certificate to Trainees

At the end of step 14, contractors shall have provided certificates of completion to trainees.

Certify trainees. After the completion of each batch of trainees, contractors shall provide traineeship certificates and/or a reference letter to trainees as proof of completion. This represents a powerful job reference for trainees. The PIU may support contractors in drafting and designing certificates (see reference letter in Appendix).

Arrange trainee award ceremony for visibility. The traineeship certificates and/or reference letters may be officially handed over to trainees at an award ceremony organized by the PIU, in coordination with TVET institutes, contractors, and political partners. The award ceremony creates political visibility, recognizes contractors for their corporate social responsibility, and provides trainees and the community with a sense of achievement.

Assess trainee (optional). In some cases, traineeships may count toward students' formal qualifications, and TVET institutes may want to conduct student assessments to confirm learning outcomes. It is the responsibility of TVET institutes to coordinate such assessments. The traineeship certificate and/or a reference letter as proof of completion shall be provided by contractors regardless of any student assessment.

STEP 15   Collect Evidence, Trainee Feedback, and Provide Certificate of Recognition to Contractors

At the end of step 15, the PIU and/or executing/implementing agency shall have provided contractors with a certificate of performance. Key tasks in this step are summarized in Figure 14.

Contractors must provide evidence for traineeship delivery as basis for disbursements. After the delivery of traineeships, The PIU verifies that traineeships have successfully taken place to certify the disbursement. Contractors shall submit evidence for successful delivery of traineeships and request for disbursements. Proofs of completion include attendance logs, proof of allowance payment to trainees, and progress reports (Table 6). Detailed information for managing disbursement is provided in the *Build4Skills Practice Guide for Procurement Practitioners*.

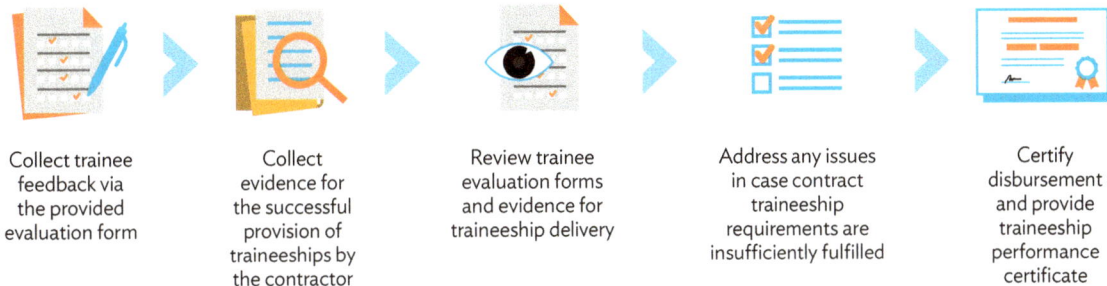

Figure 14: Key Tasks to Be Implemented in Step 15

Collect trainee feedback via the provided evaluation form

Collect evidence for the successful provision of traineeships by the contractor

Review trainee evaluation forms and evidence for traineeship delivery

Address any issues in case contract traineeship requirements are insufficiently fulfilled

Certify disbursement and provide traineeship performance certificate

Source: Author.

The PIU collects trainee feedback to independently verify traineeship completion and quality.

In addition to the evidence submitted by the contractor, the PIU is encouraged to collect feedback directly from trainees after the completion of the traineeship through a trainee evaluation form (template provided in the Appendix). The responses provided directly by trainees enable the PIU to independently verify that contractors met the traineeship contract specifications regarding (i) providing sufficient supervision, (ii) ensuring health and safety, (iii) paying trainee stipends, and (iv) employing trainees in relevant technical work areas. If the results of the evaluation do not confirm the delivery of traineeships according to specifications, the employers may follow up with contractor for clarification and corrective actions. In addition, the results of the evaluation may be stated in the contractor certificate of recognition.

Good practices when collecting trainee feedback.
The employer collects trainee feedback immediately at the completion of traineeships. The contractor cannot collect the feedback due to a conflict of interest. A good practice is to require trainees to submit the evaluation form before they receive their traineeship certificate of completion. A template trainee evaluation form is provided in the Appendix. The form includes five questions related to traineeship delivery quality that trainees are requested to answer on a four-point Linkert scale (totally agree, agree, disagree, totally disagree). The use of a Linkert scale ensures that replies are uniform and provide clear evaluative responses.

Provide contractors with a certificate of recognition for traineeship delivery.
After collecting evidence for traineeship delivery, the PIU may provide contractors with a certificate of recognition to recognize contractors' commitment to traineeships. The certificate is intended as a certificate for corporate social responsibility and is unrelated to disbursements. It exclusively assesses the contractor's delivery of traineeships, not construction-related activities. The traineeship certificate of recognition shall state (i) the total number of traineeships that a contractor has provided and (ii) optionally, the results of the trainee evaluation form as measure for traineeship quality (see next paragraph). A template certificate of recognition is provided in the Appendix. The certificates may be handed over to contractors at an award ceremony to publicly recognize the contractors' social responsibility. The lead contractor is responsible for the subcontractors and shall therefore receive the certificate.

Prepare the contractor certificate of recognition. The PIU may use the contractor traineeship delivery assessment form (Appendix) to assess contractors' traineeship delivery performance. The contractor assessment form documents the total number of traineeships provided and quality of traineeships based on the results of the trainee evaluation that can be expressed as performance statement as outlined below. The assessment form is in the Appendix, includes additional instructions for assessors, and may be used for project documentation.

1. X% of trainees agree that they worked on tasks that matched their educational background.

2. X% of trainees agree that they received instructions from contractor staff helping them to perform tasks effectively.

3. X% of trainees agree that health and safety instructions by contractor staff created a safe working environment.

4. X% of trainees agree that they received a traineeship allowance as agreed in the traineeship contract.

5. X% of trainees agree that the traineeship has significantly improved their skills and knowledge.

Arrange new traineeship batches. After the completion of one traineeship batch, a new batch may be arranged as long as the construction phase is ongoing. This means that steps 6–15 are fully or partially repeated. If contractors request new batches in new construction areas, new partner TVET institutes may be required. In cases where contractors request a new traineeship batch in the same work area, only new traineeship agreements are needed. The PIU is responsible for asking contractors to request new traineeships in a continuous and timely manner (step 8) and for coordinating arrangements (steps 7–15).

APPENDIX: TEMPLATES

List of Templates

Template	Step Where Template Is Used	Template User and Recipient
Build4skills concept note	1	Client
Indicators of ADB's Corporate Results Framework	3	Project team
Frequently Asked Questions (FAQs)	6	Bidders
Build4skills information sheet	7	TVET institutes
Request for trainees	8	Contractors
Cooperation agreement	10	Contractors and schools
Agenda for traineeship contract meeting	11	Contractors and schools
Traineeship contract	11	Contractors and trainees
Trainee certificate	14	Contractor / Trainee
Trainee evaluation form	15	PIU / Trainee
Contractor traineeship delivery assessment form	15	PIU
Contractor certificate of recognition	15	Contractor

ADB = Asian Development Bank, PIU = project implementation unit, TVET = technical and vocational education and training.

Build4Skills Traineeships Concept Note

(OneADB teams provide concept note to the client and add it to the project documents)

A. Rationale

The Asian Development Bank (ADB) is committed to supporting its developing member countries in delivering quality and inclusive infrastructure as promoted in the G20 Quality Infrastructure Investment Principles[1] and ADB Strategy 2030. Quality and inclusive infrastructure recognizes that in the age of the Sustainable Development Goals, it is not sufficient to only deliver hard infrastructure—infrastructure projects also need to create social impacts, such as employment and skills development, for communities. Given the economic opportunities that are generated by infrastructure investments, projects have the inherent potential for employment and skills development activities. Due to a prior lack of structured approaches, projects often do not purposefully incorporate such opportunities into their project design.

To unlock this potential, the ADB Human and Social Development Sector Group, in cooperation with the German Agency for International Cooperation (GIZ) commissioned by the German Federal Ministry for Economic Cooperation and Development (BMZ), has developed the Build4Skills approach. The approach promotes the provision of traineeships to local youth on ADB-supported construction sites. The focus is on traineeships as they are considered the gold standard in teaching technical skills, and empirical evidence confirms its effectiveness in helping youth transition into labor markets.[2]

The Build4Skills approach recommends that ADB-supported infrastructure projects make the delivery of traineeships[3] a contract requirement in civil work contracts requiring contractors to provide traineeship opportunities to local youth. The underlying idea is that infrastructure projects can generate wider societal benefits through a simple change to procurement requirements, resulting in significant outcomes for youth and communities including, (i) improving youth's skills and transition into jobs, (ii) connecting contractors to skilled talents from the local labor market, and (iii) enabling clients to enhance a project's inclusiveness and reputation.

B. Expected Benefits

By integrating traineeships into the project, the executing agency creates on-the-job learning opportunities for local youth and develops the local workforce in the construction sector for future public works. All stakeholders potentially benefit from their engagement in traineeships (Table 1).

---

[1]   G20 Principles for Quality Infrastructure Investment.

[2]   T. Bolli,. M.E. Oswald-Egg, and L. Rageth. 2021. Meet the need: The role of vocational education and training for the youth labour market. *Kyklos*. 74. pp. 321– 348.

[3]   The terminologies of traineeships, on-the-job training and work-based training may be used interchangeably. All confer that training takes place at the workplace.

Traineeship Potential Benefits

Stakeholder	Potential Benefits
Executing and/or implementing agency	• Additional social benefits for target community • Improved project reputation in the local community • Alignment of project with global best practices for quality/inclusive infrastructure • Improved quality of local workforce in the long term
Contractors	• Improved access to formally trained and, hence, productive workers • Improved reputation in the local community • Improved competitiveness in future bids that assess the social track record of bidders
Training institute	• Work-based training opportunities for its students • Improved capacity in cooperating with companies
Community	• Improved technical and workplace skills of the youth • Improved employability for jobs

Source: Asian Development Bank.

C.   Traineeship Delivery Modality

The Build4Skills traineeships are delivered as part of infrastructure projects. In practice, this means traineeships are delivered on project construction sites through construction contractors in line with traineeship specifications set by the project implementation unit (PIU) with the support of ADB. By leveraging these existing resources in a project, traineeships can be delivered cost-efficiently and aligned with the principles of on-the-job training.

To bestow the responsibility for the delivery of traineeships to contractors, traineeships are made a contract requirement in selected civil work contract packages. This approach enables clients to leverage their procurement purchasing power, allows project teams to efficiently integrate traineeships into the project design, and engages contractors as on-site trainers.

D.   Procurement Approach

During project preparation, the OneADB team and procurement consultants, together with the executing and/or implementing agency, identify in the strategic procurement plan report which civil work contract packages are suitable for incorporating traineeships. In principle, traineeship requirements can be incorporated into individual civil work contract packages that have (i) a contract value of at least $500,000, (ii) a construction period of at least 12 months, and (iii) a construction site located near technical and vocational education and training (TVET) institutes.

The integration of social considerations, such as traineeships, in procurement builds upon the *Sustainable Public Procurement: Guidance Note on Procurement* of ADB.[4] There is no fixed approach on how to integrate traineeships into procurement. Projects can decide what they deem to be the most suitable approach,

---

[4]   ADB. 2021. *Sustainable Public Procurement: Guidance Note on Procurement*.

whether making traineeships mandatory, voluntary, or a competitive requirement. It is recommended that projects follow the *ADB Build4Skills Handbook* and *Build4Skills Practice Guide for Procurement Practitioners.*[5] Generally, traineeships are to be included in the specifications as well as bill of quantities of suitable civil work contract packages.

E.   Stakeholder Responsibilities

Traineeships are implemented in coordination with three key stakeholders: contractors, the PIU, and TVET institutes. The PIU defines traineeship requirements, monitors if these requirements are met and compliant with contract specifications and manages related disbursements. The PIU may also facilitate the cooperation between all stakeholders. Contractors deliver traineeships as per contract requirements and specifications. It is the responsibility of contractors to proactively plan, coordinate, and deliver traineeships in collaboration with TVET institutes. Local TVET institutes assist in the student selection and placement process.

ADB provides the PIU with the *Build4Skills Handbook* as well as the *Practice Guide for Procurement Practitioners,* which outlines how PIU staff can effectively manage and coordinate traineeships.

F.   Funding

The integration of traineeships into the project design requires a marginal increase in the project budget. Traineeships are funded through the project loan by integrating costs in the bill of quantities of suitable civil work contract packages. To determine an appropriate traineeship budget, the project may follow one of the two approaches suggested in the *Build4Skills Practice Guide for Procurement Practitioners.* The traineeship budget shall only fund trainee stipend, insurance, and personal protective equipment. Other potential costs related to traineeships (e.g., instructor labor hours, work material, and occupational health and safety training) are not eligible. Those other costs are expected to be marginal and would be incurred by contractors regardless. Contractors may incorporate or subsume those other costs in other parts of their bids.

In addition, it is recommended that $1,500 for capacity development of contractor staff be added to the project budget for each year of construction.

G.   Traineeship Conditions

To ensure a safe and decent traineeship environment, projects and its contractors commit to provide the same occupational health and safety conditions to trainees as to any other construction workers engaged on the construction sites, in line with applicable safeguards and national regulations.

---

[5]   ADB. 2024. *Build4Skills Practice Guide for Procurement Practitioners.* Manila.

Key conditions of traineeships include:

(i) **Target group.** Local youth enrolled at a TVET institute or recent graduates. Where appropriate traineeships opportunities for female students shall be promoted.

(ii) **Training.** On-the-job training supervised by a contractor staff.

(iii) **Duration.** Typically, 6–12 weeks, depending on opportunities on construction sites and availability of students.

(iv) **Formal traineeship.** Contracts detailing the traineeship terms and conditions, signed by each trainee.

(v) **Stipend.** Stipend and/or other provisions such as food and transport allowances for each trainee.

(vi) **Safety.** Application of safeguards and standards, including providing insurance, appropriate personal protective equipment, and the required occupational health and safety training for each trainee during the traineeship.

(vii) **Certificate.** A certificate of completion and/or reference letter provided to trainees.

Indicators of ADB's Corporate Results Framework Relevant for Build4Skills Traineeships

(Project teams may include these indicators in project documents)

OP	Pillar	Level	Sub-Pillar	Results Indicator	Tracking Indicator
1	1: Human Capital	2	Learning opportunities for all improved	1.1 People benefiting from improved health services, education services, or social protection (number)	1.1.1. People enrolled in improved education and/or training (number)
1	2: Quality Jobs	2	Labor standards and policies strengthened to enhance the work environment	1.2 Jobs generated (number)[a]	1.2.3. Enhanced labor policies or standards implemented (number)
2	2: Gender equality in human capital enhanced	2	Women and girls' participation in nontraditional education and training increased	2.2 Women and girls completing secondary and tertiary education, and/or other training (number)[b]	2.2.1. Women and girls enrolled in STEM or nontraditional TVET (number)
6	1: Improved public and corporate sector management functions and financial stability	2	Capacity of public institutions to promote private sector and financial sector development improved	6.1 Entities with improved service delivery (number)	6.1.2. Measures supported in implementation to improve capacity of public organizations to promote the private sector and finance sector (number)

OP = operational priority; STEM = science, technology, engineering, and mathematics; TVET = technical and vocational education and training.

[a] "Jobs" refers to activities that generate income, monetary or in kind, and follow standards of decent work as defined by the International Labour Organization. Build4Skills traineeships are recommended to be remunerated and should stress the importance of occupational health and safety training, traineeship contracts, and provision of insurance, and therefore may be counted under this indicator.

[b] "Other training" includes nontraditional technical and vocational education and training, and other types of formal or informal training, full-time or part-time. Build4Skills traineeships may be classified as "other training" and typically concludes with the provision of a certificate through the contractor.

Source: Author, based on ADB. 2022. *Results Framework Indicator Definitions*.

TEMPLATE
Frequently Asked Questions About Build4Skills Traineeships (for Bidders)
(Project implementation unit and procurement consultants may provide the FAQs to bidders during tendering to address any questions)

General Information

What is the Build4Skills traineeship requirement?
Build4Skills is a contract requirement in Asian Development Bank-supported infrastructure projects that requests contractors to provide traineeships to local vocational education students on construction sites. Contractors are expected to deliver traineeships as outlined in the contract specifications.

How many traineeships do contractors need to provide?
Contractors are requested to deliver as many traineeships as specified in the bidding documents.

What is the role of contractors in Build4Skills?
Contractors are responsible for providing on-the-job training on their construction sites. Company staffers supervise and instruct trainees, and coordinate traineeship placement with local training institutes.

What is the role of the PIU in Build4Skills?
The project implementation unit (PIU) monitors traineeships and may facilitate cooperation with local technical and vocational education and training (TVET) institutes.

What Are Traineeships?

What is a traineeship?
In a traineeship, TVET students receive on-the-job training directly at the workplace of a company, supervised by company staff. While learning, trainees also perform productive tasks.

How long is a traineeship?
Minimum 6 weeks, maximum 12 weeks, depending on student availability and opportunities on construction sites as determined by the contractor.

In which work areas do traineeships take place?
Contractors decide in which work area trainees are needed and can be assigned. It must be in technical areas and may include jobs such as binders, welders, electricians, concrete workers, etc. Jobs such as helper or security guard are not recognized as a traineeship.

When should traineeships be delivered?
Traineeships can be delivered throughout the entire construction period and in multiple batches. This is decided by the contractor, but it also depends on the availability of students as indicated by TVET institutes.

Traineeship Expenditures

What are the key expenditures associated with traineeships delivery?
The key eligible expenditures are trainee stipend, accident insurance, and personal protective equipment (PPE).

Selecting Partner Schools and Recruiting Trainees

How are traineeships set up?
Contractors shall arrange traineeships in cooperation with local TVET institutes. This partnership can be set up via a cooperation agreement that the PIU can help to set up.

Where are trainees recruited from?
Trainees come from local TVET institutes that offer training programs that match the traineeship work areas requested by contractors.

Who selects partner schools?
The contractor identifies suitable TVET schools. The PIU may suggest partner schools to contractors.

Who selects trainees?
Schools select students whose qualifications match the skill profiles requested by contractors. Upon request, the contractor can take part in the selection process.

Who is eligible to be a trainee?
Any student enrolled in a construction-related training program or a recent vocational education graduate, who finished a relevant program less than 6 months before the traineeship begins. It is strongly encouraged to create equal opportunities for male and female students to be a trainee.

Drafting Traineeship Contracts

What are traineeship contracts?
Traineeship contracts specify the exact terms and conditions of traineeships and are signed by the contractor, trainee, and their TVET institute as well as, where applicable, legal guardians of trainees.

Who decides on the conditions in the contract?
Contractors, together with TVET institutes, decide on the details and conditions in the contract while considering any relevant and applicable laws.

Implementing Traineeships

Who delivers traineeships?
Contractors, represented by their on-site instructor (company staff), deliver traineeships. The on-site instructor guides and instructs trainees on how to implement work tasks.

How are traineeships regulated in practice?
The traineeship contract regulates how traineeships are delivered, including hours and times, areas of work, leave of absences, etc.

What does a trainee do on a construction site?
Trainees shall contribute to regular tasks on the construction site in line with their ability and assured of their safety.

What happens after traineeships?
The contractor provides a certificate of completion to trainees. Upon satisfactory performance, the contractor may decide to work with the trainee in the future.

Contractor Performance Assessment

Is the performance of the contractor for delivering traineeships assessed?
Yes. At the end of the contract, the PIU assesses the traineeship performance of contractors and provides contractors with a certificate of recognition.

How is the contractor's performance reviewed?
The PIU follows a standard assessment procedure, evaluating two criteria: the number of traineeships delivered and trainee feedback.

Traineeship Program Information Sheet for Technical and Vocational Education and Training Institutes

(Project implementation unit shares the information sheet with local training institutes to inform about traineeships)

Who are we?

We are the [Project Name] supported by the Asian Development Bank. The [Project Name] is implemented by [Name of key local institution] and has construction sites in [Name of regions, cities or districts] from [year-year]. We are active in the [Urban/Energy/Water/Road/etc] infrastructure sector.

We offer traineeship opportunities on our construction sites!

Under the project, our contracted construction companies offer traineeship opportunities to local vocational education students on our construction sites. This is an opportunity for students to gain work experience and improve their technical skills.

We are looking for vocational training institutes that are interested in providing their students with traineeship opportunities!

What can trainees expect?

Our traineeships last 6–12 weeks. Trainees will engage in supervised traineeships and receive a certificate from our contracted construction company. The exact traineeship details, including dates and traineeship areas, are determined in discussions with our construction companies.

Who can become a trainee?

Technical and vocational education and training (TVET) students with a relevant educational background can participate in our traineeships. The ideal candidate is a final year student (or a recent graduate) in a construction-related qualification program, with good social skills and the maturity required for a professional construction site. Male and female students are welcome to apply.

Call to Action

If you are interested in providing your students with a real workplace learning experience, let us know.

Please e-mail or call our coordinator

[Name of e-mail holder, e-mail, Telephone number] and include the following information so we can connect you with upcoming opportunities:

(i)   Name of TVET institute

(ii) Contact person

(iii) List of qualification programs in construction-related professions you currently offer

TEMPLATE

TEMPLATE
Request for Traineeships Form

(Project implementation unit shares the form with contractors to collect information about upcoming traineeship opportunities)

Company Name:
Name of Contact Person:
Office Address:
Phone #:
Email:

Dear Project Implementation Unit Team,

We are writing to inform you about the upcoming traineeship opportunities on our construction site in accordance with procurement requirements that stipulate the provision of traineeships. Details on traineeships are outlined in the table below.

We kindly request you to assist us in identifying trainees with the required qualification background and to put us in contact with these potential trainees and their schools.

Occupational Area of Traineeship (e.g., welding, electrician, concrete, etc.)	Period of Traineeship (dd/mm/year – dd/mm/year)	Number of Trainees Required	Location of Traineeship

We are looking forward to providing opportunities to local youth for more inclusive infrastructure.

_____

Place, Date, Signature

TEMPLATE
Cooperation Agreement
(Project implementation unit may use the cooperation agreement to support contractors and TVET institute to formalize their partnership)

Preamble

The cooperation agreement is signed between:

Party 1, hereinafter referred to as *the Company*

Name of the company:

Name of the signatory, position:

Contact Number:

Address:

Party 2, hereinafter referred to as *the TVET institute*

Name of the TVET institute:

Name of signatory, position:

Contact Number:

Address:

Purpose

The Company and the TVET institute aim to cooperate on delivering traineeships on construction sites contracted to the Company under the Asian Development Bank (ADB) project [Project Name]. Traineeships will take place in multiple traineeship batches over the period of the cooperation agreement. The purpose of the cooperation agreement is for the Company and the TVET institute to agree on the general cooperation modalities for the delivery of traineeships.

The cooperation agreement shall be valid from the day of signing until the completion of the Company's contract with the ADB-supported project [ADB project name] on the [Date].

General Cooperation Duties

The Company will receive students as trainees on the construction site(s) contracted to them for a duration of 4–12 weeks; supervise and instruct trainees through its own technical staff; and provide each trainee with a reference letter or certificate of completion upon successful completion of the traineeship.

The TVET institute will identify suitable students and make them available to participate in traineeships; support setting up traineeships in line with current TVET regulations; and fully inform prospective trainees' parents/guardians about traineeships and request their consent if required.

Cooperation Outline

Preliminary Traineeship Venues

The Company confirms that the construction sites where traineeships can take place are as follows:

#	City, Street	Type of Construction
1	[e.g., Makati, Bel-Air Street]	Wastewater infrastructure
2	[e.g., Quezon City, Tree Street]	Office tower construction
3		
4		

Preliminary Traineeship Dates

The Company confirms that traineeships can, in principle, take place in the months indicated in the table. The TVET institute confirms that students are, in principle, available to participate in traineeships in the months indicated in the table.

The TVET institute and the Company agree that the ideal traineeships dates are the months of X, Y, Z.

All parties acknowledge that the timing for traineeships can be affected by unforeseen circumstances.

	Jan	Feb	Mar	Apr	May	Jun	Jul	Aug	Sep	Oct	Nov	Dec
Construction site availability for traineeships												
Student availability for traineeships												

Note: Months marked with (x) indicates that traineeships can take place on construction sites or students are available for traineeships.

Preliminary Traineeship Occupational Areas

Given the civil work contracted to the Company under the [ADB project name], the Company anticipates that over the course of the construction period, traineeships can be offered in the following occupational or work areas:

Occupational Area	Anticipated Dates (if known)	Location (if known)
e.g., Welders	Year(s)/month	e.g., Makati
e.g., Binders	Year(s)/month	e.g., Quezon City

Request for Trainees

Traineeships take place in multiple batches over the course of the construction period. The Company will regularly provide to the TVET institute the number of trainees required for a given traineeship batch. The Company should make timely requests to ensure a feasible planning horizon for arranging traineeships.

Selection of Trainees

The Company and the TVET institute agree that prospective trainees are selected jointly or directly by the TVET institute.

The TVET institute will promote traineeship opportunities among its students with a focus on final year students and recent graduates (graduation not more than 6 months ago). The TVET institute will only pre-select students that have the aptitude to successfully engage in traineeships based on a high level of maturity, social skills, and technical aptitude.

Traineeship Contracts and Delivery

The Company and the TVET institute agree to formalize traineeship details in traineeship contracts that are signed by the Company, the TVET institute, and each of the prospective trainees at an appropriate time in the future.

Both parties agree to ensure that trainees will have a stipend, accident insurance for the duration of the traineeships, necessary personal protective equipment for the construction site, occupational health and safety training prior to the traineeships, and appropriate supervision during the traineeship. Both parties share the responsibility for finding feasible solutions to fulfill these measures and document them in traineeship contracts.

Next Steps

The Company and the TVET institute agree to take the following next steps:

- The Company will provide a detailed request for trainees (if it has not already done so).
- Suitable students are selected according to the process agreed upon in the cooperation agreement.
- Traineeship contracts are agreed upon and signed with prospective trainees.
- Traineeships are delivered.

TEMPLATE

Traineeship Contract Discussion: Meeting Agenda

(Project implementation unit may use the meeting agenda to set up a structured discussion between contractors and TVET institutes about traineeship details)

Objective: Agree on traineeship details for final traineeship contract draft
Date:
Participants: [Contractor X, TVET institute X, PIU staff X]
Note taker: ...

Agenda Items

Topic	Guide Questions	Time in minutes
Introduction	Meeting objectives and participants	5'
Section 1: Training/work area	In which field of work will the traineeship take place? Is there a need for a structured traineeship plan?	5'
Section 2: Duration	How long is the traineeship? And on what dates will it take place?	5'
Section 3: Traineeship location	At which construction site and address will the traineeship take place?	2'
Section 4: Stipend and other provisions	How much stipend will the trainees receive? When will the trainees receive their stipend? Does any party provide transport and/or food services to the trainees?	10'
Section 5: Work safety and accident insurance	Who will cover the accident insurance of the trainee? Is social insurance also required? Who will provide occupational health and safety training? What personal protective equipment is required and who will provide it?	12'
Section 6: Training hours and leave	What are the trainees' regular traineeship hours? On what weekdays do they report to the construction site? How many leave days are trainees entitled to? How do trainees inform the contractors about sick leave?	12'
Section 7: Certifications	Who certifies the completion of the traineeship? Will the trainee receive a certificate and/or reference letter? What information must be included in the certificate of completion and/or reference letter?	10'
Section 8: Obligations of the company	What are the general obligations of the Company?	10'
Section 8: Obligations of trainees	What are the obligations of trainees during the traineeship?	10'
Section 8: Obligations of the TVET institute	What are the obligations of the TVET institute?	10'
Section 9: Termination of contract	What are the procedures if a party wants to terminate the contract?	5'
Section 10: Dispute resolutions	What are the procedures to resolve any potential disputes?	3'

TEMPLATE
Traineeship Contract
(Project implementation unit may use the traineeship contract to support contractors, trainees, and optionally also TVET institutes to sign well-drafted traineeship contracts)

Preamble

This contract is concluded between:

Party 1, hereinafter referred to *as the Company*

Name of the company:

Name of the Signatory, Position:

Contact Number:

Address:

Party 2, hereinafter referred to *as the Trainee*

Name of the Trainee:

Name of Trainee's TVET Institute:

Contact Number:

Address:

Party 3, hereinafter referred to as *the TVET institute*

Name of the TVET Institute:

Name of Signatory, Position:

Contact Number:

Address:

Section 1 - Purpose

The purpose of the contract is the training of the Trainee in the occupation X through an on-site traineeship at the Company. For this contract, "traineeship" is defined as a form of vocational training that takes place in a real-world environment for the development of technical and work-readiness skills. [if applicable] It focuses on skills agreed upon by the Company and TVET institute which are outlined in the training plan in the annex.

Section 2 – Duration of Training

The Trainee, trainee name, will participate in the traineeship for the period dd.mm.yyyy – dd.mm.yyyy.

Section 3 – Traineeship Venue

The traineeship is offered by the Company and takes place within the context of the construction works contracted to the Company as part of the ADB-supported infrastructure project [ADB-supported project name]. The traineeship location is at the following address:

[Full address]

Section 4 – Stipend and Other Provisions

1.   Stipend

The Company will provide the Trainee with a weekly/monthly stipend of X (local currency) for the duration of the traineeship. The stipend is directly paid to the Trainee at the end of each month/weekly.

The Company agrees to continue to provide the stipend to the Trainee in case of sick leave of X days or less. If the Trainee is absent from the training site longer than X days due to sick leave, the stipend may be paused.

2.   Other Provisions

[if applicable] The Company will provide food for lunch... [if applicable] The Company will (not) provide transportation to the construction site from the TVET institute, and from the construction site to the TVET institute.

Section 5 - Work Safety and Insurance Coverage

1.   Personal Protective Equipment

The Company or the TVET institute will provide the Trainee with the personal protective equipment (PPE) required to perform the traineeships safely. The Company shall determine which PPE is required.

2.   Occupational Health and Safety Training

The Company or the TVET institute will provide the Trainee with occupational health and safety training as required for performing the traineeships safely.

3.   Accident Insurance

The Company or the TVET institute will provide the Trainee with an accident insurance for the duration of the traineeship.

Section 6 – Training Hours and Leave

1. Training Hours

The daily trainings hours of the traineeship shall last X hours per day in line with the TVET/Labor Law X. The regular working hours that the Trainee shall spend at the construction/learning site are between 0:00 a.m. and 00:00 p.m. on the following workdays: Monday, Tuesday, Wednesday, Thursday, Friday. The Trainee is entitled to a daily break of X minutes.

Upon request and in agreement with the TVET institute, the Trainee may be asked to attend the traineeship site on alternative weekdays in compliance with the labor/TVET law.

2. Annual and Sick Leaves, Unexcused Absence

Leave days: The Trainee is entitled to X leave days per month. The Trainee shall inform the instructor about planned annual leave at least 1 week in advance.

Sick Leave: In case of sickness, the Trainee shall inform the instructor or the Company's front office as well as the TVET institute about sick leave in a timely manner.

Unexcused absence: The Company shall report an unexcused absence of the Trainee to the TVET institute. After two documented warnings due to unexcused absence, the Company may terminate the traineeship contract in consultation with the TVET institute.

Section 7 – Certification

At the completion of the traineeship, the Company will provide the Trainee with a certificate of completion or reference letter. The reference letter or certificate is provided as a hard copy to the Trainee. It must, at the minimum, include the name of the Company, name of the Trainee, duration of traineeship, occupational area where on-the-job training took place, and signature of a Company representative. At the discretion of the Company, it may include details on the conduct and performance of the Trainee.

(If applicable) The TVET institute confirms that the traineeship is recognized toward the formal qualification program that the Trainee is enrolled in, earning the Trainee X credits.

Section 8 – Obligations of Parties

The Company

The Company shall fulfill the following obligations:

(i)   Fulfill the conditions and provisions as outlined in the sections of this agreement.
(ii) Assign and make available a staffer as an instructor who has the personal and technical aptitude to supervise and instruct the Trainee.
(iii) Entrust the Trainee only with tasks that match the Trainee's qualification background.

(iv)   Instruct the Trainee on any internal regulations of the Company and construction site at the beginning of the traineeship.

(v)   Provide a safe and healthy working environment to the Trainee in line with national laws and safeguard requirements of the given contracted work. This also includes an environment that is free of harassment, psychological pressure, and discrimination.

(vi)   Inform the TVET institute about notable incidents during the traineeship, including accidents and conflicts.

(vii)   Not impose any fees or costs, including costs related to damage, on the Trainee other than stated in this agreement.

(viii) (Optional) Sign trainees training logbook.

(ix)   (Optional) Be part of the assessment board led by the TVET institute.

The Trainee

The Trainee shall fulfill the following obligations:

(i)   Fulfill the conditions and provisions as outlined in the sections of this agreement.

(ii)   Comply with the rules of conduct and safety procedures of the Company and the training venue at all times.

(iii)   Follow the instructions of the instructor(s) and designated coworkers.

(iv)   Perform the tasks entrusted to him/her diligently and handle tools, machinery, and other equipment with care, using them only for purposes as instructed.

(v)   Act responsibly and respectfully at all times.

(vi)   Inform the instructor about a planned leave at least 1 week in advance.

(vii)   Not miss days of training without a valid reason and inform the instructor about sick leave or other reasons for his/her absence, indicating the prospective date of return.

(viii) Assure confidentiality about the Company's internal information.

(ix)   Follow the traineeship plan and working hours.

(x)   (Optional) Document all training tasks performed in a logbook and collect any signatures from instructors if required.

The TVET Institute

The TVET institute shall fulfill the following obligations:

(i)   Fulfill the conditions and provisions as outlined in the sections of this agreement.

(ii)   Nominate a focal point that can be directly contacted by the Company and the Trainee to address any matters related to the traineeship.

(iii)   Prepare and inform the Trainee about challenges and appropriate behavior at a construction site before the start of the traineeship.

(iv)   Monitor attendance of the Trainee.

(v)   Mentor and advise the Trainee on all matters related to the traineeship to ensure the Trainee's well-being.

(vi)   Mediate between the Company and the Trainee in case of complaints or disagreements.

(vii)   Optional, develops jointly with the Company a traineeship plan.

(viii) Optional, arrange the assessment and certification after completion of the traineeship.

Section 9 – Termination of Contract

The Trainee and the Company may terminate the agreement at any point with notice. Notice of termination must be given in writing to all contract parties.

The traineeship opportunity can, in principle, be transferred to another student in a separate new traineeship agreement if requested by the Company.

Section 10 - Dispute Resolution

All parties shall address any potential dispute in a cooperative manner. If disputes cannot be directly resolved between the Company, the Trainee, and the TVET institute, the project implementation unit of the name of the ADB-supported project may be consulted for arbitration.

[Company, Name of signatory]   [TVET Institute, Name of signatory]   [Trainee, Name of signatory]

Place, Date: Place, Date: Place, Date:

------------------------------   ------------------------------------   -----------------------------
                                                                          [Trainee's legal guardian, Name]
                                                                          Place, Date:

Traineeship Plan (optional)

This traineeship plan is agreed between the company and the technical and vocational education and training (TVET) institute and shall guide the assigned in-company instructors in overseeing the traineeship.

Week	Work Areas / Key Assignment	Further Comments
1	For example: • Introduction to the work environment (tools, locations, colleagues, etc.) • Introduction to work ethics / company rules (including working hours, breaks, communication) • Health and safety instructions	
2	Performing oxyacetylene welding: • Practice personal and equipment safety • Assemble work material. • Prepare work material. • Performing setup, adjustment of flame and gas pressure, and shutdown.	
3	Performing oxyacetylene welding: • Plan welding approach to accomplished desired result. • Manipulate torch at proper angle. • Perform assigned welding job.	
4		
5		

TEMPLATE
Reference Letter for Trainees
(Project implementation unit may share with contractors the reference letter for trainees template to support contractors in providing reference letters to trainees)

[Date]

[Trainee's name] has completed work-based training at [company's name] in [location] from [starting date] to [end date]. [Trainee's name] was engaged to perform the following tasks:

[task 1]

[task 2]

[task 3]

[task 4]

During this period, the trainee has demonstrated competence and knowledge in the tasks assigned to them by the company's instructor. The trainee was always present at the assigned infrastructure site or informed the instructor in the case of absence. They demonstrated good communication skills that helped them get involved with the team, and they are nice person to work with. We would recommend them for further training/work in their profession/occupation.

If you need additional information, please contact me via email: [Company's Email / Instructor Email]

[Name of Company Instructor / Name of HR responsible]

_____

Signature

TEMPLATE
Trainee Evaluation Form

1. Each trainee must fill out this form providing truthful information.
2. Individual responses will not be shared with contractors.
3. Do not write your name on the form. The feedback is anonymous.

Instructions: *Please respond to the following questions in writing.*

Basic information	Answer
Today's date dd/mm/yyyy	
Where did your traineeship take place? *City*	
Which contractor did you work for? *Name of contractor*	
In which occupation did you complete the traineeship? *Name of occupation*	
Which training institute / school are you attending? *Name of school or TVET institute*	

Instruction: *Please indicate your level of agreement with the following 5 statements by drawing a circle around the answer, like the example in blue.*

Example	This traineeship form is easy to fill out	Strongly agree	Agree	Disagree	Strongly disagree
Statement 1: In my traineeship, I worked on tasks that matched my education background.		Strongly agree	Agree	Disagree	Strongly disagree
Statement 2: At least once a week, an instructor (e.g., company staff) gave me instructions that helped me to perform tasks effectively.		Strongly agree	Agree	Disagree	Strongly disagree
Statement 3: Instructors (e.g., company staff) ensured that I always followed safe working practices and conditions.		Strongly agree	Agree	Disagree	Strongly disagree
Statement 4: I received a traineeship allowance/ stipend as agreed in the traineeship contract.		Strongly agree	Agree	Disagree	Strongly disagree
Statement 5: The traineeship has significantly improved my skills and knowledge.		Strongly agree	Agree	Disagree	Strongly disagree

If you want to share anything else, please write it in the box below (optional):

You are done. Please submit the form. Thank you for filling out the form.

TEMPLATE

TEMPLATE
Build4Skills Traineeships – Contractor Traineeship Delivery Assessment Form

(Project implementation unit may use the assessment form to assess the contractor's performance in delivering traineeships and document it internally)

Key Information

Project Name and Number	
Civil Works Contract Package Number	
Name of Contractors	
Name of Person Conducting Assessment	
Date of Assessment	

The performance of the contractors is assessed by counting the total number of traineeships provided and collecting trainee feedback through an evaluation form as follows:

Assessment 1: Number of Traineeships Provided

The number of traineeships provided by the contractor is verified by counting the number of traineeship contracts signed between contractors and trainees. Alternative ways of assessing traineeships may be used.

Instructions for assessors: *The assessor shall fill in the number in the column "number."*

Assessment Item	Number of Trainees	Source
Number of traineeships provided by contractor for the given civil works contract package	*XX*	*Traineeship contracts counted*

Assessment 2: Trainee Feedback/Evaluation

The project implementation unit collects feedback from trainees through traineeship evaluation form. The results of the evaluation indicate if contractors have delivered traineeships according to all key specifications.

Instructions for assessors: The assessor fills in the table below based on the results of the traineeship evaluation form collected from trainees. To calculate percentages in the last column, the assessor adds up the number of answers that indicate agreement ("totally agree" and "agree") and divides it through the total number of feedback received. The resulting percentage (last column) indicates the rate of satisfactory performance of contractors for each of the five performance statements, which may be included in the certificate of recognition.

Statement of evaluation form	Total number trainees who replied, Totally agree	Total number trainees who replied, Agree	Total number trainees who replied, Disagree	Total number trainees who replied, Totally disagree	Total no. of responses received	Sum of "totally agree" and "agree" responses	% of trainees who responded "totally agree" or "agree"
1: In my traineeship, I mainly worked on tasks that matched my education background.							%
2: At least once a week, I received instructions by contractor staff that helped me to perform task more effectively.							%
3: Instructors (e.g., company staff) ensured that I always followed safe working practices and conditions.							%
4: I received a traineeship allowance/stipend as agreed in the traineeship contract..							%
5: The traineeship has significantly improved my skills and knowledge.							%

Summary Assessment

Instructions for assessors: *The assessor shall summarize the results of the assessment in the box below. The summary statement can be used when preparing the certificate of recognition.*

The [name of project] hereby acknowledges that the contractor [NAME OF CONTRACTOR] has provided XX traineeships.

Trainees provided the following feedback on the traineeship quality:

- X% of trainees agree that they worked on tasks that matched their educational background.
- X% of trainees agree that they received instructions from contractor staff helping them to perform tasks effectively.
- X% of trainees agree that instructors ensured that they always followed safe working conditions and practices.
- X% of trainees agree that they received a traineeship allowance as agreed in the traineeship contract.
- X% of trainees agree that the traineeship has significantly improved their skills and knowledge.

TEMPLATE
Contractor Certificate of Recognition
(Project implementation unit may award contractors with the certificate of recognition to officially acknowledge contractors' efforts in providing traineeships)

Certificate of Performance for the Delivery of Traineeships

In recognition of the social responsibility of [Name of Company, registration number], the [Name of project] hereby acknowledges that [Name of Company] has provided xx **traineeships** and received the following feedback by trainees:

- X% of trainees agree that they worked on tasks that matched their educational background.
- X% of trainees agree that they received instructions from contractor staff helping them to perform tasks effectively.
- X% of trainees agree that instructors ensured that they always followed safe working conditions and practices.
- X% of trainees agree that they received a traineeship allowance as agreed in the traineeship contract.
- X% of trainees agree that the traineeship has significantly improved their skills and knowledge.

Traineeships were delivered as part of social considerations of the contracted civil works that were awarded to [Name of Company] within the context of the [Name of project].

Name, Position

Place, Date

Signature

www.ingramcontent.com/pod-product-compliance
Lightning Source LLC
Chambersburg PA
CBHW050051220326
41599CB00045B/7370